THE PHOENIX RISING

PART II

Francy Audrey Black

DEDICATION AND SIGNATURE

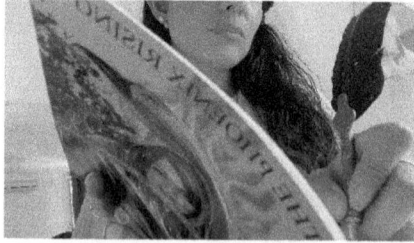

The greatest example of love is your existence, remember that there is always a reason to continue; just look around you, and then you will see that what happens is never bigger than your existence. You are the great miracle of life. "FAB"

Copyright © 2025

Author: **Francy Audrey Black "FAB"**

Special editing and correction in English by:

Carolyn O'Connor

Edited by:

Enrique Kook & Ricardo Montaña

Cover and design:

Alberto Ariza and Manuel Malaver, Luis Celis

Contribution:

Kylee Honeman & Paola Ramos

ISBN: 978-0-6486138-2-4

It was 6:20 pm on 13th October 2020, an unforgettable day. My last memories of what was once my life are of walking to the second floor where my meeting with destiny awaited me. I remember noticing a resident coming toward me. The next minute I felt a heavy, painful blow to my head, and everything went black.

AS MY CONSCIOUSNESS FADED AWAY, I SCREAMED TO MYSELF, "MY GOD, WHAT IS HAPPENING?" SUDDENLY, EVERYTHING WENT DARK AND SILENT. I FELT A PEACE I HAD NEVER EXPERIENCED BEFORE. IN THE MIDDLE OF THE DARKNESS, AN IMAGE OF THE LOVE OF MY LIFE APPEARED. SHE STOOD UNDER A LAMP, THE LIGHT SHINING ON HER, SHE WAS ALONE, SHE WAS THERE WAITING FOR ME.

Table of Contents

Welcome to the Phoenix Rising

Hi to everybody who has decided to begin this journey with me. I believe that every book, no matter what type, has a purpose in the life of whoever is reading it. I hope that when you are reading "The Phoenix Rising" you too can find a personal message.

The Phoenix Rising book is about the big new adventure that I am starting now. In both books I write about different situations and the feelings that these situations awaken in me. Something I learned from The Phoenix Part I "Not available in English version yet" is that a book is nothing if it does not have a reader who will experience the incredible, amazing, sad, romantic, dramatic and happy stories that are shared in it. When you read this book, it would be wonderful if you could immerse yourself in this incredible but also dramatic story, make it yours and take something from it for yourself.

As I write this, I feel so happy and lucky to keep sharing my story with you.

Writing a book is complex, even when you don't have any obstacles or health issues. Trying to write it after suffering a Traumatic brain injury and having constant health issues is a roller coaster that tests my endurance and perseverance.

In the first book, The Phoenix Part I "Not available in English version yet" I wrote about the situations I experienced earlier in my life, how these situations made me who I am today, and the reasons that brought me to Australia.

You do not need to read the first book " The Phoenix Part I" to begin this second book, " The Phoenix Rising" as I have included a summary of the more important topics from the first book, to help you better understand this book.

The events in this book are based on my experiences, although the names of people and places have been changed to protect their privacy. It is important to mention that "The Phoenix Rising" is based on my perspective and opinion, which is related to what I have experienced on this new journey that life has given me. With all due respect, everyone has their own perspective and opinion, and my intention is not to influence or change that.

You will find sections where I focus not so much on the facts but on my own experience of them. For this reason, my recommendation is to focus on both of the above, so as not to lose the story in the book.

In Dedication To...

"This path is full of challenging ups and downs but in the end, all of these situations have a reason to be in our lives. "FAB"

This book belongs to all the people who have supported me in the recovery process. To my beloved family, to my doctors, and specialists and to all the other people who have been by my side during this time. To my mother for being so brave and crossing the world for me, to my daughter, who is undoubtedly my battery in the days of downfall. To Enrique Kook for his editing, participation and support in the books.

To organisations such as **ROMERO CENTRE, AMPARO Advocacy, RAILS, Indooroopilly Uniting Church, Latin Manna, Hope restaurant, Sports and Spinal Woolloongabba, Herston Private Hospital, Doctor F. Jaramillo, Phycology Ivannia, Prof. Carlos, Psychiatry Tran, Staff de Kenmore Clinic,, ABIOS, Mater Hospital, Miss Shilleena, Queensland Health Victim Support Service y Henderson Centre.**

To all my supporters, and for the donations and pro bono you have made, which have allowed me to pay for part of my therapies. Thank you to all of you who read the first volume, and who want to know what has happened since then. This second volume is written for you. I want you to know that each one of you has played a fundamental role in my recovery process and my life.

Every person who came into my life in this process taught me something and showed me life in different shapes and colours. Their messages of love, their prayers, their emotional and psychological support, and the financial contributions have given me the opportunity to pay for my therapies and other expenses. Without a doubt, I have been a light bulb on the tree that has been fed by all the wonderful people who continue to pray and who, positive in the midst of the storm, lift me up every time I fall. And well, thanks also to all those who have shown me another side of the coin, placing obstacles throughout this process. Every part needs a counterpart, which measures our level of wisdom and courage.

Prologue

I met Francy almost 15 years ago when she handled the entire onboarding process of the company where I started working at that time. From the beginning, I was surprised that such a young woman was in charge of the selection and incorporation process in a big company like that, but I quickly realised it was due to her efficiency and diligence with all the things that were assigned to her.

I still don't know how or why, but a few weeks after I joined, she began to ask me with some frequency to join her for a coffee break at the corner store. I took advantage of this as a kind of "active break" in my daily work. There, we usually had some small talk about the going on at the company: The company's projects, gossip in the workplace and about our lives, and between these conversations we started asking and giving each other advice, both professional and personal. That is how we soon became close friends.

I remember that her departure from this company was a very difficult moment, because despite having a lot of experience and great capabilities, she did not have a professional degree yet, and this became an obstacle to moving forward in an industry in which many times this "nobility certificate" is practically a requirement not only to move forward but even to enter.

Thus, she sought to undertake in all possible ways, setting up from a development company with her ex-boyfriend at that time to a hairdresser with her sister. I must say that I admire her tenacity and persistence, but above all no matter what she had to do, she always did it with the best attitude and put all the drive and passion into it. Having also been an entrepreneur, I know that undertaking is a difficult bet and does not always yield the fruits we expect: For different reasons, each of these initiatives fell by the wayside, and each dream ended up coming to an end.

And there was my friend, recently separated from a complicated relationship in which, however, a thousand dreams had been woven; without being able to access a job that was comparable to what she earned in her previous job, and without a source of income that would allow her to get ahead with her daughter who, as you will read in this volume and the previous one, is basically the love of her life and the reason for getting up and continuing to fight every day.

In the absence of options comes anxiety, despair and even sadness, and they are there even when you talk to your friend and she always responds smiling, telling you that she is fine. Paths that otherwise would never have been contemplated are then explored, and when Francy told me about going to Australia, I thought she was going crazy, but as a friend I supported her (As I usually have done, even in her most difficult projects) and wished her fair winds and a following sea, asking the few contacts I have on the other side of the world to take a look at her just in case.

My friend fell in love with that country, and looked for a way to stay there, studying and looking for a job that would allow her to be productive and generate income for herself and her family. When she excitedly told me that she had found a way to coordinate with her daughter's father so that she could go with her, I was very happy for her, trusting that things would finally work out well for both of them.

How could I have imagined that soon a misfortune would befall upon my friend, harming not only her income and her probability to stay there, but even her functionality and even her life? When I found out what had happened - months after the fact -my eyes watered when I learned about what had happened, and how absent I, as a friend, had been after the fact.

I have followed her evolution from then on, keeping an eye on her health state without being able to do much from a distance other than rejoicing at her winnings and being sad about her hard moments, listening to her from time to time and encouraging her from a distance to move forward when she felt that she couldn't take it anymore.

So, when she asked me for help with something I could help her with —to edit this book about her life story and adjust it so that it can be delivered to you, dear readers —I immediately agreed. We already did that work in the first volume, which I hope you have had the opportunity to read, and here I continue, perhaps in a slightly empirical way, but with all my heart, knowing that my friend's story is worthy of being heard, and hoping that you, who are reading these lines, can find it interesting and perhaps can use its lessons for your own story.

With love,

Wolf

In The Last Phoenix

Part I book

In the "Phoenix Part I", I shared with all of you some of the different aspects of my life.

This included how my grandparents changed cities to escape the political violence and find a safe place for the family; where and how I was born and the different situations that my mother had to face in the 80s, with all of the social stigmas of becoming a single mother; and the reason I began to work at an early age to help my mother with the cost of running our home.

I also wrote about my family and friends' experiences that taught me a lot about life and how this influenced my path. I also told of how I lived with another family for a while.

I described how my relationship with my mentor, who became the most influential person in my life, opened new opportunities in my personal and professional life. I also wrote about my experiences when I became a mother and wife. I mentioned many different projects that I worked on and how I met the last person with whom I had a serious relationship, which after some time became a nightmare.

I shared about how great but challenging it is to make a choice to change everything in my life, to arrive in a new place with no knowledge of the language or culture … Australia.

And now to continue my story...

Chapter I

The Change

The Fall

Although I had arrived alone in Australia in 2017, the beginning of 2020 marked the end of my studies and was a promise of many opportunities for me and my daughter. To me, 2020 would be the best year for us. After working hard for two years and making a lot of compromises for my studies, I finally could have my daughter with me.

In my mind, everything was planned and organised. A place to be safe and live together, a job and further studies. However, I did not have any idea of what was coming, I think nobody could imagine what would happen in our world in less than four months, and definitely not something of this magnitude.

Suddenly, a terrible and unknown enemy of human life spread around the world; COVID-19 was killing millions of people everywhere. India, Italy, and Brazil experienced the greatest loss of life, as shown in the day-by-day death count released by all the news portals around the world. Most countries called for quarantine to minimise the risk of spread.

Panic invaded everything and everyone, so, my opportunity to do the internship and obtain my degree to start working as a carer or support person seemed to be slipping through my fingers.

But after I tried, on my own, to find a home care that offered the opportunity to do the internship, the college where I was doing my studies surprised our group with the news that they had a place offering internship opportunities for all of us. We were so happy about this. Of course, the emotion of everyone in the group was incredible, as we all needed 120 hours of internship before we obtained our qualification.

Expectations Vs Reality

When we arrived at the home care, we were all so happy that we could finally do our internship. We had waited for months.

Daniel was the supervisor who was in charge of training us in our roles at the home care facility. Daniel is a great person with strong values and principles. He has been working in the support care industry for many years. We were so lucky to find someone like him to support and teach us on our new path, especially because he treats people with respect, and compassion and has a lot of empathy when looking after the residents.

Depending on the personality and the values in the person's life, sometimes it will be difficult to ignore the suffering of other human beings, to keep going like life is perfect, especially for empathy and compassion. This is something really important to me... because I believe every person deserves to be treated with respect, love, compassion and dignity.

Upon our first visit to the home care facility, and seeing just the reception area, something was telling me that things were different from what the college had explained to us.

While we were being shown around the facility, the faces of my colleagues showed that they were upset. The building was the opposite of what we had expected. It was very dilapidated but not because of the supervisor or manager, it was the lack of maintenance of the structure, the floors, the furniture and other things. The truth was that the team, manager, supervisor and administration were working hard to care for the place, but unfortunately, they were very short of staff.

Many of the recommendations for improvement and maintenance requested by the team at the home care when passed on to the owner and business partners for approval were not approved.

This was disappointing as the home care service had a lot of responsibilities, such as cleaning, administering medication, providing emergency support, personal care, helping the chef during food time, cleaning beds and everything that someone needs to have to live a quality of life. All of this was the responsibility of the supervisor, who had to look after 40 or more residents alone.

The individual care plan for each resident itemised their allergies, medication schedule, dietary needs, likes or dislikes, hobbies and all the personal needs of the resident.

It is the responsibility of the supervisor to promote, aid and inspire the residents, in a respectful and caring way, to complete activities, such as exercise, meal assistance, personal care, dressing, attend personal appointments, and participate in new activities. Sometimes the supervisor would have support depending on whether students were available or not. When a resident requires full support, the supervisor needs to provide all primary care. Everyone needs to follow the moral or legal responsibility, as outlined via the principle of 'Duty of Care', a commitment that we decide to take on when we become a Support carer.

In our studies, we were trained to support and care for

the clients, patients, and residents, considering their emotional, psychological and physical needs, guiding the person to be autonomous in the different areas of their life, to guarantee the quality of their well-being.

We, students, had to learn a wide variety of other important tasks, such as the use of equipment to assist lifting, moving, walking aids, pack padded bed transfer, emergency calls, assistance in case of emergency, first aid and other tools that support the client in day by day living. We, as carers, are not allowed to assist with medication or injections unless we had been trained for this task. If the client is unable to be independent, the carer needs to support them with feeding, showering, changing incontinence aids, cleaning the house, cooking, laundry, grocery shopping, etc.

However, in the home care where we were doing our placement, we were not going to be able to practise even 80% of what we learned in the course. Honestly, it is rare that a person can practise everything they studied!.

Nevertheless, I felt that although it would not be an easy job, eventually with much effort and perseverance the place could be improved before everything inside those walls consumed us alive.

Once we had completed our workplace training and introduction, we were then required to develop a roster based on our availability.

Once we were outside the Home Care, I said to my colleagues, 'There are two things here', the first is that I know it is not what we expected, and the second is, this place has a lot of potential. If we work together, we can show that we are ready to work in this field.

They all looked at me and smiled. After this everyone went home. I drove home with Rocio, the only other person that speaks Spanish. Our conversation was about the different things that we had seen in the care home and the expectations of what our group had to try to practice. She cheered up.

The Home Care, where we were going to do our internship was a Level Three care service facility. For example, it is something similar to a home for aged care but specialised in the treatment of people with mental conditions and physical disabilities. Not all of the residents live with mental problems or disabilities. According to our training and what the administrators of the Home Care told us, a level three home is a house where these residents are offered personal care such as meal assistance, medication and emergency care, among other basic needs.

We would be integrating these skills into our daily practice. Our responsibilities were to take care of these residents and ensure a healthy, safe and clean environment for them. Obviously, at the same time always maintaining emotional and professional distance from them.

This was not easy for me. Looking after residents as a

home carer is an incredible and rich experience, but in this situation, I could see and understand what their lives were like. The hard reality was that most of the time they were sad and lonely. Usually, the residents were with other residents, but rarely did any of their family or friends come to visit them. Seeing the residents in this situation made me feel a lot of empathy and compassion for all of them.

Daily work with the residents involves seeing them on their sad days, happy days, quiet days, sick days, and other situations. Seeing them alone and without family somehow made me feel affection and compassion for them. Talking to some of them revealed to me the heartbreak they carried. I felt an infinite loneliness, melancholy and desolation as a result of working there. Depending on a carer's personality, not feeling empathy is almost impossible. Working with the residents day by day made me feel more and more that they were part of me. Confusing, right?

My job as a professional was never to judge the residents, as for why they were there. It was for those months of practice, I concluded that they deserved more than just care, as a person needs love, respect, patience, compassion and dignity.

However, not everyone thought or felt the same way I did. One of the things that struck me during my placement was the lack of empathy from some of the staff for these residents. I remember a day when one of the residents told the chef that they could not eat what was on the menu. He asked for a sandwich. The chef answered that it was not his problem, and if the resident could not eat the food provided then the person could go to bed hungry.

I witnessed this incident! In response, I decided to go to the kitchen, and made the resident a sandwich to eat for dinner. Minutes later the angry chef told me 'I should not have given the resident a sandwich'. My answer was easy...'My understanding is, if the residents pay for a service, then it's their right to receive it.

I told him if he sent people hungry to bed or denied them

services it was not ethical or right and that he was not doing his job or letting me do mine. My opinion was that if he was unhappy working with them, he was maybe working in the wrong place. After that, he looked at me and went away.

Many situations like this, and others happened during my time working there. I reported them, however the person in charge never did anything. Some of the staff abused the residents in different ways such as denying food, being aggressive towards them, and punishing them. They were creative in finding ways to make the lives of some of these residents unbearable. Obviously, nobody talked about this.

Two days before I ended my placement, I had a call from the manager's office, asking me to go to the office. When I arrived, there were four people waiting for me. Their faces were serious, so I thought something was wrong. However, the manager told me they had recommended me for a position that was available in another house. The HR person explained the role, saying that the team thought my work on placement was great and that if I was interested, I could start as soon as possible.

My heart stopped! It was the most amazing news that I could have had. I was trying to find an extra job to earn more income because our visa had to be renewed in a short time. I looked at them and I said that of course, I was happy to accept the offer.

It was like a dream had come true. The work was near my home so I could coordinate my time between jobs, house responsibilities, studies and the more important responsibility of being a mother. This was a big achievement, securing a job before my placement had ended.

However, sometimes things don't happen as we are planning or expecting. Destiny, God, Karma, any name we want to give it, had different plans for me.

It was 6:20 pm on 13th October 2020, an unforgettable day.

My last memories of what my life once was, are of walking to the second floor of the Home Care Facility, where my meeting with destiny awaited me. I remember noticing a resident coming toward me. The next minute I felt a heavy, painful blow to my head, and everything went black.

*As my consciousness faded away, I screamed to myself, "My God, what is happening?" Suddenly, everything went dark and silent. I felt a peace I had never experienced before. In the middle of the darkness, an image of the love of my life appeared. She stood under a lamp, the light shining on her, she was alone, she was there **WAITING** for me.*

The First Hours

It was about 7:15 pm when I opened my eyes. I did not know where I was, except maybe that I was on the floor; everything was spinning around me, my head was throbbing, it was difficult to breathe, and the pain was overwhelming. I was confused, and disoriented, when I tried to sit up, my body did not respond. I tried three times. Each time I tried, panic and fear set in. I could not feel my body, so tears rolled down my face … I was alone with no one around to help me.

The fourth time I closed my eyes and took a deep breath. Suddenly, in the midst of the pain, the confusion, the despair, she appeared again… my daughter. This time, when I tried to sit up, I finally managed to do so. Using the little strength I had left I forced my body to stay upright while tears ran down my face. I opened my eyes again and it was then that I finally knew where I was. On my right was the food dispenser machine.

The pain throughout my body was excruciating (especially on the right side), my head was throbbing like never before. I could not move until long after I understood where I was.

I remember in the middle of my confusion I put both of my hands on the floor and slowly crawled up to the wall on my left. I stayed there for a few minutes and then, leaning on the wall, I managed to stand up. Everything hurt; my head was pounding, I could not breathe, everything was spinning. Then I closed my eyes again and said to myself " Oh my God! What happened to me? Did I slip? Did I faint? What's going on?"

After some time, the supervisor on duty came to the corner where I was leaning. He was with someone else. I remember him asking me what had happened. I replied, " I do not know, but I am in a lot of pain and feeling dizzy." The guy told me to sit down and left.

As I sat there, I saw the person who assaulted me; he was on the other side of the table sitting next to other residents. His gaze was cold and intimidating as if he were no longer himself. His face was transformed by fury, and it scared me a lot. My heart raced even faster. I looked at the wall to try to escape his look. Then I saw the clock. It was 7:35 pm. "Oh my God! My daughter!" Then I found strength from deep within myself and started walking.

The next thing I remember is looking at myself in the mirror in the reception area in front of the manager's office. It was there that I realised that something very bad had happened to me. As I looked in the mirror, I noticed that both sides of my face were bruised, but the right side was particularly swollen and purple.

I was having trouble breathing and couldn't move my right arm properly. One of the residents was sitting there, looking at me with a tender expression and asking me if I was okay. I looked at him and said yes. He asked again, "Are you sure?" I insisted that I was. At the same time, the Supervisor rang me and asked for my incident report. I told him I was on my way to do it.

The next thing I remember was the call I made to Christian, with whom I was in a relationship at the time.

"What happened, love?"

he asked, hearing me crying.

"Something happened to me and I don't know what it was,"

I said. "Everything hurts, I can't breathe, and my head is pounding like it's going to explode."

He asked:

"Where are you?"

"In the car," I replied.

"How? Didn't anyone help you?" he asked indignantly.

"My daughter is alone waiting for me," I said, ignoring his question, "and your daughter too."

He sighed and said, "Honey, when you get to your daughter, tell her to call me."

From there, I only remember stopping at red traffic lights, before reaching my daughter, about 15 minutes later.

She got into the car and said, "Mom, it's cold. I thought you forgotten to pick me up,"

I tried to contain myself but burst into tears. The pain at that moment was unbearable.

She looked at me, scared, and said:

"Are you okay, mommy?"

"Baby, something weird happened to me and I don't know what it was," I told her. "Everything hurts."

She told me:

"Let's go to the house and call an Uber and we'll go see Eliana" (my boyfriend's daughter). I said okay.

Two or three minutes after we started driving, I couldn't move anymore. My position in the car was causing me excruciating pain throughout my body and making it impossible to breathe.

I told my daughter:

"I need you to take the wheel and help me get the car to the house." I gasped.

She put on the parking lights, and I moved my foot as much as I could to slowly move forward until we reached the house.

Once there, I tried to get out of the car, but my body

would not respond. My daughter was very scared and called Chris, who told her:

"Leave her in the car if you can't get her out and call the ambulance."

At about the same time, the supervisor called me, scared, and said,

"I need you to come back. One of the residents assaulted you and said he did very bad things to you. He thinks he killed you."

I replied that I couldn't move. By then I was crying from the pain (And saying 'crying from the pain' after giving birth to my daughter, I assure you, is equivalent to a 15 on a pain scale of 1 to 10).

I don't know how she did it, but my daughter pulled me out of the car. When the paramedics arrived, they gave me morphine and immediately took me to the hospital. My daughter was crying out of fear because she saw me in such a vulnerable state.

That night, she stayed with a friend. A very nice family

who had supported me a lot, especially during the night shifts, taking care of my daughter.

Chris, who was eight hours away by car, was distressed because the paramedics had told him that I was in critical condition and that they did not understand how it was possible that I had not been helped at work. He rushed to the airport in anguish, but he could not get a plane ticket, so he rented a car and drove back in the middle of the night, worried and desperate, hoping to see me. It was about five in the morning when I felt his hand touching mine while he was kissing them and crying. I remember him pleading, "I love you, don't go."

I opened my eyes, looked at him tenderly and whispered, "'It's not going to be that easy to make me leave you."

He smiled, kissed my head and asked:

"How do you feel?"

"I'm in a lot of pain," I mumbled, "but less than I was 8 hours ago. I feel confused, drugged and I can't breathe very well."

He then explained the situation to me

"You have a broken bone in your face. Your brain, chest and arm are swollen. They don't know what happened to you, but they say that you must have been attacked very viciously."

After leaving the hospital, Chris called the company manager. And He told them:

"Her jawbone is broken, her brain, chest and arm are swollen, and who knows what else," he shouted, bursting with anger. "You guys are irresponsible!"

That was when they responded that they were going to file a report. Of course, at that point, they hadn't gone to the police station yet.

"I'm going to the police station in an hour," Chris replied angrily, "and I'm going to mention your negligence in my report."

I remember the conversation well because Chris wasn't talking. He was yelling.

When we got home, he lifted me out of the car and carried me upstairs. He tried to lie me down on the sofa, but I started choking. I couldn't breathe. On top of that, I couldn't drink water or anything else. I couldn't move my mouth. Chris was very concerned and upset because I was completely drugged by the medication they had been giving me during The First Hours in the hospital.

In time, Some relationships will come to an end

Chris asked for 15 days off to look after me. As time passed the symptoms only got worse. I could barely speak, I couldn't understand him or my daughter, my memory started to fail me. I would then get confused and repeat tasks. I couldn't sleep. I was in a sitting position all the time because otherwise, I could not breathe.

Ten days later we had an appointment to see if I was going to have surgery on my face. The swelling had gone down. The Plastic Surgeon looked at the X-ray and said he thought it was best to wait 6 months before making a decision.

Then Chris mentioned,

"She's also complaining about her ribs or her chest. She's not sleeping, and she says she's in a lot of pain."

The Plastic Surgeon looked at the X-rays and, to the surprise of all three of us, said,

"She has a broken rib and another fractured rib. That's causing the pain she's complaining about."

Chris got mad. This time, before he could speak, I looked at him and said, "Let me speak."

Then I turned to the doctor and asked, indignantly,

"What kind of doctors ignore something like this?"

"I'm sorry," he said.

"The hospital staff who treated you were students who are doing their internships."

I just looked at him, not believing what I was hearing.

"The pain I'm in doesn't allow me to breathe or sleep or eat," I told him.

Chris added,

"She's not sleeping, she repeats tasks she's already done, she doesn't talk, she walks weirdly and every time she hears any noise, she panics.

I've heard her crying a lot, she's very distressed and she's not normally like that. What's going on with her?"

The Plastic Surgeon looked at us and said, "I'm sorry, she needs a neurologist, a good GP to oversee her medical treatment. What she's been through and is going through is not and will not be easy to recover from. However, with the right medical care and specialists, she will get through it."

My six-month relationship with Chris ended a month and a half after the incident.

Chris's last words to me, while tears fell down his cheeks, were, "I do not know what is happening to you. I do not know how to help you. I am just watching you fall apart and into an abyss without being able to do anything for you"

I looked at Chris and said," Go away, for both, yours and my wellbeing. I should keep going with my journey on my own."...Some relationships will come to an END!

After Chris left, everything got worse. The symptoms were terrible, and now I was dealing with all this alone. I did not mention anything to my daughter, my friends or my family. I was feeling afraid, sad, confused, and embarrassed. I isolated myself in my room, only coming out to get food before returning and locking my door. I was living in hell.

It was like I was living in a movie. I didn't understand what was happening. The dizziness, the passing out, the falls and the migraines got worse. I felt a burst in my head, which I can only compare to when you hit yourself so hard and you're left seeing lights. These pains became stronger and more frequent and that made me vomit from the pain.

My nose started to bleed. I had fainting spells. I began to feel that my body was losing strength. The carer, organised through my GP, to help me with things around the house mentioned to me one day that I was walking strangely. I began to think that I was going crazy.

The RED appointment

As the weeks and months went by, Acquired Brain Injury Outreach Service (ABIOS), who had seen me twice in the hospital started taking an interest in my treatment. They contacted my Workplace Insurance company recommending that I see a physiotherapist, speech pathologist and a psychologist. After several months my GP also started requesting the recommendations of ABIOS be put in place by Workplace Insurance.

Once I started being treated by these specialists, they all started to mention that I needed to see a neurologist urgently. Among them was Rachel, my speech therapist, who repeated this at every appointment. "Francy, you need to see a neurologist."

It was strange, as she kept repeating this request at every appointment, so I mentioned it to the GP who was following my case, who was not satisfied with the progress I was making.

My GP referred me to a neurologist, but I remembered that this appointment – or any other referral or examination I had to undergo – had to be approved by the Workplace Insurance.

So I decided to go to Workplace Insurance to ask for their support.

When I started the claim with the insurance company, I had an advisor called Camila, who was very committed to my case. She was so kind and concerned about my health. However, one day, for no apparent reason, Camila wrote to me saying that someone else would take over my case and that she wished me a speedy recovery. Two days later I received a call from the new person. Laura. Her voice was not friendly. She introduced herself and ordered me to terminate my treatment with the territorial brain injury department or ABIOS, and then she hung up.

After this call, my nightmare had just begun. A few days later I had an appointment with Marcela, the occupational therapist in the brain injury department ABIOS. While I was in the waiting room, I was talking to an interpreter. I told him in Spanish about the call I had received.

He looked at me and said, "Take my advice, For your own good, Do Not, close your ABIOS case. This insurance company is used to ripping off people without anyone being able to do anything." He added, "They do it to permanent residents, they do it to citizens, and now you can imagine what will happen to someone in your situation."

When I entered Marcela's consulting room, I told my interpreter: "I want you to tell her that I received a call from the insurance company ordering me to close the case here."

At that time my English had deteriorated greatly due to the brain injury, and I was barely speaking. I did not need to speak English to see the disagreement on the therapist's face after the interpreter told her this.

Then she looked at me and through the interpreter she said: "No. We are not going to close your case with us and you are not going to close it either. What is the reason they gave you?"

"I do not know," I replied.

Then she looked at the interpreter and through her she said to me: "Your case is not easy; your situation is very complex. For many reasons, you need to continue to be treated and monitored by us and I will write an email asking why they want you to close the case with us."

The following week I had a visit from Cristian, the occupational therapist from the insurance company. During this visit I had a friend who could help translate. Cristian arrived, sat down, and introduced himself. Before he asked me anything about my health, the first question he asked was, "Have you already informed the brain injury department that you will not be continuing with them?"

I asked my friend what Cristian had just said?... Then I looked him in the eye and said, "No. I'm not going to do that, and there's no reason for you to demand or ask me to do that. On the contrary, they are giving me some services that have helped me, so I'm not going to cancel them. This is my health we're talking about."

After that, Cristian's attitude changed. He asked me a few questions and quickly left.

I suspect that it was on that day that I, signed up for 'what would be the beginning of the end' my personal war with the Workplace Insurance, since from that moment on the new advisor, Laura, began to make my life impossible.

Laura denied Doctor's requests, cancelled appointments, stopped insurance payments, and removed the few services that the previous consultant had arranged to help me, and generally did whatever she wanted, with my case.

Laura even denied me the right to have an interpreter, which in Australia is a Human Right, that must be fulfilled to ensure that the person can understand in their language what is happening. This is to promote equality for people who speak English as a second language.

I continued to try and receive decent treatment for my condition, but many of my requests for testing or referrals were initially denied.

I confirmed this with my doctors, but they let me know that they couldn't do anything unless the insurer approved the tests.

The emails started to get very provoking and unpleasant, and I, with my poor English, continued to respond to them, telling them that I was only asking for appropriate medical treatment to be able to continue with my rehabilitation. Several doctors and specialists had intense calls with Laura, all requesting support for my treatment. The advisor and manager ignored everything and everyone. Laura did "whatever she wanted" with me and with everyone.

To explain the claims process, at the beginning of the claim, the employer must send the information about what happened to the relevant insurance company to qualify for the claim. The Workplace Insurance then decides whether or not the case qualifies for the claim process. If the insurance company accepts the claim, a process begins with the doctors and specialists who access the person with a suggested treatment and recovery plan.

Each case is handled differently and has an advisor assigned by the insurer. The job of this advisor is to ensure compliance with their policy which (theoretically) is to help the person recover safely, and in a timely manner so that they can return to work as soon as possible. Once this has been achieved, the case can be closed and the payment that the Insurance Company must make for the medical treatment, plus 75% of the insured's wage at the time of injury, can be finalized. (At least, this was to be the process in my case).

So, while I was at my worst physically, psychologically and emotionally, plus it was getting worse every day, the Workplace Insurance was telling me that my case was going to move to the closing stage and that, as a consequence, the (inadequate) treatment I had been receiving until then was going to end. Now, to clarify, in order to close a claim, the person must have been examined by the Workplace Insurance's specialists, and after that, their case must be reviewed by the Workplace Insurance Tribunal.

As a result, I decided to let my employers know everything that was happening with the Workplace Insurance, as there was no way I could possibly go back to work.

That day, despite the mental confusion caused by the brain injury and my poor English, I took the time to write an email to my employers. It took me 10 hours to put it together. I tried to explain to them that I thought the way the insurance company was handling the case was irresponsible and negligent.

So, I started by listing all the issues that had arisen since Laura had become my advisor. I mentioned that she was dismissive in her emails to me, that, although I had asked for the interpreter service, she had denied me that right. I explained I had complained to the Insurer that many times I felt discriminated against, plus there was an element of racism in her dealings with me, and as this is prohibited by law in Australia under the Human Rights Commission and the Anti-Discrimination Act, I asked that Laura be removed as my advisor. Their response was to threaten me. All of the above could be backed up by evidence from the various emails I had written to the Insurer and copied to the doctors.

Interestingly, up until that day, all the reports from the insurance company said that I needed more medical treatment and that I was not yet ready to return to work. However, when I had the appointment with Simon, a doctor hired by the Workplace Insurance, he - in a very literal role of devil's advocate - immediately asked me: "Are you being advised by a lawyer or a law firm?". This question seemed rather irrelevant and out of place in a medical interview, especially after I had been seen by more than 20 doctors and specialists, so I didn't answer it and moved on to the next question.

This appointment was different from previous

appointments,

specially the questions and the way the doctor addressed me. At the end of the appointment, he said, "You have a Traumatic brain injury, post-concussion, plus other issues."

I asked: "Doctor, how long will it take for the dizziness, fainting, and other symptoms to clear up?"

"I don't know," was his response.

Before I left the office, the doctor asked again about the lawyers. I looked at him and said categorically, "NO."

Five days later, I got a call from Daniela, the person who had my case in the brain injury department or ABIOS.

"Did you check your emails from last night?" she asked me.

"No," I said. "I really don't want to read anything from Laura. Today is not a good day." "Then don't do it," Daniela said. "Can I come by tomorrow afternoon and we'll talk?"

I answered "Yes".

At the time I didn't know it, but Simon had issued a report contradicting all the other doctors who had seen me, including the other doctors from the Workplace Insurance, and requesting that the case be closed in 2 months.

The next day, in the morning, I had an appointment with the specialist Soraya from the group of private doctors (not from the insurance company).

"Francy, they can't close the case if you're not stable and you haven't had treatment," she told me.

I looked at her in surprise and said in my mind: "GOD! What happened?"
"You didn't know?" she asked.

"I saw the email, but I didn't read it," I told her.

"It's better that you didn't read it," she replied.

Soraya went to the Workplace insurance website and started reading through each link. She was looking for something. I didn't understand what it was until she opened a Word document and started writing an email in English.

She explained that there was a clause or policy in the Workplace insurance contact that gave me the right to request that another specialist of the same category as Simon evaluate me urgently.

I did not accept the diagnosis of this last doctor, since he was the only person who thought that I should return to work without taking into account the other reports or my health status.

In the afternoon Daniela arrived from the Acquired Brain Injury Outreach Service (ABIOS)

"Did you read the email?" she asked me again.

"No," I said, "but this morning I had an appointment with Soraya, and she told me that they were going to close the case."

I showed her the email that Soraya wrote.

"Did you send it?" she asked me.

"Yes."

Daniela asked: "Share the email with me, please."

———————————————————————

The email did not work as I had at first hoped. Laura, the advisor, managed to close the case with lightning speed and send me back to work as I was, which only made my health worse.

The migraines got worse, the dizziness became more constant, and everything just got worse. Still, I needed to work, not just to occupy my mind, but to bring in some money I said to myself,

"... I can do it, I can do it."

The irony of this situation is that I wasn't ready, and my body was getting worse. I would go back to the Home Care, work. Sometimes I would have a nosebleed, or I would run to the bathroom to vomit from the pain, and my health began to decline more and more in every aspect. The mobility problems also got worse, my body was aching, and migraines were increasing.

Sometimes my colleagues would ask me: "Why did you come back to work?" "You look tired?" "Do you feel bad?" However, as we say in Spanish, "a need has the face of a dog". If I didn't work, I wouldn't have the money to pay rent, food, etc., since up until then I was a casual worker.

In the end, I exploded. I wrote to the insurance company, with a copy to the doctors who were treating me, telling them that if something happened to me, they would all be directly responsible, for the situation I was in, and as a result my declining health, since I had been asking them all, to provide help since the event happened (2020).

I pointed out that Laura, the advisor in charge of my case, ignored all requests, made from the doctors and specialists, Laura again denied The red appointment, and the Neurology.

Pressures and Depressions

With the ongoing pain, symptoms, post-trauma, and multiple panic attacks that followed, the infamous depression and anxiety also appeared.

I began to fall into a very deep depression. I kept telling everyone that something was happening, but no one could tell me what I had or give me a diagnosis that explained all my symptoms. However, everything was like a downward spiral. I forgot almost everything, and the little I remembered was from the diary I was writing.

Until that moment in my life, I really had not understood what depression was. That feeling of emptiness, fear and hopelessness. It's like nothing was worth it anymore; the feeling that I was being crushed like an insect and that, no matter how much I fought against that feeling of loneliness and sadness and, above all, emptiness, I could do nothing against it.

The thoughts of suicide came, each day stronger and more tempting, as if I were no longer in control of myself. It was as if that emotion controlled every second of my days and my life.

So, I called my best friend back in Colombia, Ricardo, and standing on the balcony of my room, crying, I sobbed:

"I want to kill myself! I want to end this pain that is driving me crazy. I can't take all this!"

I remember him telling me: "Beautiful, you are stronger than you know and everything that is happening is very complicated. Please don't do anything."

Then days and nights under surveillance began by him, through eight to nine-hour phone calls, to prevent anything from happening.

However, things did not change. One day I went to the physiotherapist and was upset. I started crying and told him: "Something is wrong, this is not normal, and no one is listening, this is real to me." He tried to calm me down, but when that didn't work, he asked me: "What is going through your mind?"

"I want to kill myself right now," I told him. "It's over. They (the Workplace insurance) won."

To this, he replied: "I need you to see a psychologist or a psychiatrist right away. We need someone to take care of you for a while."

After talking to him, I picked up my cell phone and called the occupational therapist at the Workplace insurance. I said, "I'm in a crisis. I need help and I need you to do something now."

He said he would try to speak to the case manager. However, he informed me that he could not do anything. I remember yelling at the occupational therapist in a way that shocked the physio. Until that moment I had never behaved like that. After finishing the call, I left the physiotherapist and went to the psychologist.

I remember arriving at the psychologist's office and

telling her that my mind was completely out of control.

She looked at me in surprise and even a little alarmed.

"I have these ideas stuck in my head and they are not good," I continued. "I don't know what is going to happen. It's not me."

"I know, Francy," she said. "The physio called me, and I think he also wrote to the insurance company."

She invited me in and asked: "What's wrong?"

I started to cry.

"Everything is wrong!", I sobbed. I freed myself from my fear of being misunderstood and judged and told her about all the things that had been happening to me both physically and mentally, and that I had not shared this with anyone due to this fear.

"I hurt all over, I faint, I can't breathe, my head explodes, and I don't remember what I'm doing. I feel sad and this sadness doesn't want to go away. I don't even know what's happening to me. I don't want to continue with this macabre game with the insurance company. I don't understand how the insurance company is putting me in this situation, even though I am a human being. My daughter is suffering, and I can't help her. I can't even help myself."

Then the psychologist gave me a bottle of water and said: "Let's calm down."

After talking, she picked up the phone and called the insurance company. She told the lady who answered the call that I was in a risky situation.

"She is not well," she told her, but the person from the insurance company in turn gave her a million excuses and, in the end, came up with nothing.

I don't know if perhaps my continuous requests, complaints and claims, together with those of the doctors and specialists who were treating me, generated too much pressure on the insurance company.

What I do know is that after looking for every possible way to ensure that I would be denied any medical service, the insurance company ended up opting to call the police.

While I was still with the psychologist, a police officer rang me. I burst into tears and told her, "This is just a result of pressure, lack of responsibility, and the treatment that the Workplace insurance refuses to give. Now they want to avoid responsibility by calling the police.

Tell me what I did wrong. All I did was go to work that day, to help other people, and now neither the Workplace insurance nor my employers want to take responsibility for my treatment."

The officer was silent. "Francy, everything is going to be okay," she finally said. "I'm so sorry to hear about what you and your daughter are going through," she added.

She then asked me to put her through to the psychologist. My psychologist spoke to the officer for a few minutes and when she hung up, she looked at me and said: "I couldn't get any support to take care of you. So, we better admit you at the hospital."

I looked at her and said: "It can't be possible that I now have to go to a hospital as if I were to blame!" I said, frightened. "And my daughter? What is happening to her? She needs me! "The psychologist looked at me, bewildered and sad. "We must find a solution," she told me.

We spent hours waiting to find someone since I didn't have many friends and the few I had I was embarrassed to admit and tell them what was happening. Finally, we found a friend I had worked with before, who could help me and stay with me for a few days, especially at night.

For obvious reasons, I didn't want to be left alone with my daughter. In retrospect, I have realized that I didn't trust myself. So the psychologist drove me to my house, left me with my friend and then talked to her for a few minutes. Before leaving, she said to me:

"Francy, think about your daughter, your family, your friends and the people who are trying to help you... I know it doesn't feel that way, but everything will get better. Nothing is forever and you can be sure of that."

The Ambush

Days went by and sadly my condition did not improve. During this time, unbeknown to me, the insurance company requested that the police do another safety check on me. And that is what happened.

One day, when I arrived home after one of my medical appointments, I found three police cars and two ambulances waiting in the driveway of my house. A police officer looked at me and said, "We were waiting for you."

"Why?" I asked.

"We have a red flag in your case file," the officer replied.

I invited her to come into my house. She sat down across from me and we started talking. I told her everything that had happened with my health and insurance since the attack.

"I've done everything as instructed," I said. "Medications, appointments, everything. However, I'm asking for an appointment with a neurologist because something isn't right. I'm fainting for no apparent reason, the pain is excruciating, I'm having trouble speaking, thinking, moving, and now they're using you as if I were a criminal, to cover up the disaster of how the Workplace insurance, and especially this consultant, are handling the case."

She looked at me, clearly embarrassed or upset by what I had told her, and said, "I know." adding "Francy, I don't see a bad woman in your eyes. I don't think you are dangerous at all. On the contrary, it is surprising that after 18 months of the attack, you are still fighting for your daughter and for yourself. However, I think you should let yourself be helped by us, as the Workplace insurance is placing you in a very difficult position".

I looked at her and tears started pouring out of my eyes like it was raining in torrents.

"The paramedics need to check you out and with your help, they will decide what we are going to do," she told me.

The paramedics (a man and a woman) who had been at the entrance listening to everything, came into the room and said: "Francy, we sympathize with what you just said. It's so sad to see you in this situation when it is clear that you were helping others and now you are the one who has to pay the consequences of this."

Then the paramedic intervened and said: "We need to take you to the hospital and evaluate you physically and psychologically."

At that moment I said, "My God! Now they are going to lock me up in a mental hospital! What about my daughter? What will happen to her?"

But then I looked at him and for the first time, I realized that I had to let myself be helped. Even though I knew that it was not a mental problem, I decided to accept the help.

The next thing I knew, I was in the ambulance. The officer asked me, "Do you have someone you trust who can take care of your daughter?"

"Yes," I replied.

She called my daughter's friend's family, and they—sad about everything we were going through—spoke to the officer.

The mother told her: "We have known her for two years, she is a good mother and a wonderful person. Whatever she is going through just breaks our hearts. Of course, we will take care of her child. She is like another daughter to us."

When I got to the hospital, the paramedic spoke to me and explained.

"You need to go to the Psychiatric Ward," he said. "You'll be there for an evaluation. You need to be honest with the psychiatrist and everything will be fine."

I looked at him as I entered this part of the hospital. I felt so bad and sad. How was it that after having studied, worked and had a happy life, I was now sitting there?

I asked myself. What had I done wrong?

Then the psychiatrist called my name and asked me to follow him.

"We have the email from the Workplace insurance company saying that you are at high risk of committing suicide, or something worse happening," he told me.

I looked at him.

"Doctor," I said, "I don't know what's going on, but up until two years ago I had no physical or mental health problems. I began to have health problems after the assault and they have suddenly worsened, as you can see for yourself by reviewing my medical records.

You can't expect me to be okay with this, after everything the Workplace insurance has done to me. They now have sent the police to sanction me in order to keep me quiet and stop me asking for more medical treatment. This is the only thing my doctors and I have asked for, which is fair given the circumstances in which I obtained the injuries. So, Doctor, I feel that the insurance company is using you. It is obvious that their purpose is to get me admitted to a psychiatric hospital to evade their responsibility."

The doctor looked at me and said, "Sorry to hear this but everything is going to be okay, Francy. We are going to keep you here tonight for observation."

Then, he sent me to a high security ward with six small rooms. I was alone in a room with no phone or personal contact apart from when the nurse checked on me.

I cried all night. The Workplace insurance had broken me. They had destroyed the emotional and psychological stability of both me and my daughter. They were playing with my health. They had put me in a difficult financial situation, not to mention other difficulties that came as a result of the assault.

They had caused me to be locked up and now I had even lost hope. I felt like I was worthless. Like my daughter and I were nothing more than little insects that you just step on with your foot and no one will say anything about it.

The next day Daniela, the brain injury specialist from ABIOS, who was in charge of my case, arrived. She looked sad, but when she saw me enter the room she stood up, hugged me, smiled and said: "I brought you a hot chocolate with soy milk and this book with a message from your daughter that said: I love you, mommy, we are going to be very fine.

"I'm glad you're okay," Daniela continued, handing me the things. "I spoke to your psychiatrist, and he told me that he's going to transfer you to the clinic where his practice is situated so he can keep a closer eye on you. It's a better place than this one, and your daughter will be able to visit you."

"I'm so sorry, Francy," she said. "I am. I know you've tried everything to get through this. It will only be for a few days," she finished. "I promise to call your daughter every day... I'll call you and visit you if I can."

Around noon I was transferred to the new clinic.

When I arrived, Erick, the psychiatrist, came into the room.

"What happened?" he asked me.

"I don't know," I said. "What I do know is that the Workplace insurance did this."

He looked at me and said, "I've never seen a situation

like this." He didn't look happy. "They can't just send the police to you and treat you like that,"

So, I raised my face and said, "I'm an immigrant in this country. I'm nothing to them, and they can apparently do whatever they want with us."

He sat down in front of me, and said, "Francy, neither they nor anyone else can take away your dignity or worth as a person. Only you can do that."

"I'm going to keep you under observation for a couple of weeks," he explained to me. "We'll give you regular medication that will make you sleep. I need you to recover because lack of sleep is very serious. Anyway, your daughter can come here to visit you."

He continued "When you get out of here you should be ready to continue fighting for yourself and your daughter. In all my years of experience, I have never come across a person like you. You are brave, you are intelligent, and you love your daughter and your family. This is not going to stop you. You will get through this; you have no other options. Do you understand what I am saying?" I looked at him and nodded.

These words and similar support from my physio, the GP, the psychologist, the psychiatrist, and others, were what gave me strength and courage. Every time I felt broken, one of them looked me in the eyes and gave me a word of encouragement. Despite the giant obstacle that the insurance company had become, they continued to take care of me, and today I can say that thanks to these wonderful people that I am here, writing these lines.

The Uncertainty...

While I was hospitalized at this clinic, Daniela, the brain injury person from ABIOS, came to see me and told me, "I made an appointment with Laura, the advisor, and with Laura's Manager. I told them I didn't agree with the way you are being treated. Especially by Laura. I don't like the way she is handling your case, and from what I see, you requested a change of advisor a while ago, but nothing happened. I didn't see a response to that email."

I answered, "They didn't respond,".

I know for a fact that a few days later Daniela, who was my support person, had an appointment with Laura, the advisor, and with Pablo, Laura's direct manager.

There is one thing I can assure you. The person who came back from that meeting was not the same person who had been supporting me previously. For some strange reason, I began to feel that these people from the Workplace insurance company intimidated almost everyone, and my question was, Why? But the answer I got some time later was even more surprising. The insurance company is run by the state government.

That's when I understood everything: Laura, the advisor, had made all her moves very well and had finally beaten me

However, I repeat. Although I do not belong to any religion, I do believe in a higher being, in the laws of the universe and justice.

It had been three months since I returned to work, and by that time I had already been hospitalized several times due to constant fainting spells, when the appointment with the new specialist from the Workplace insurance arrived - a doctor named Julian.

When I entered, I gave him evidence of all the medical reports, along with photos of the bruises and damage my body experienced every time I fainted. I remember that this appointment also made me feel uncomfortable because when I entered the consulting room, the doctor asked several tricky questions and performed several physical exams on me.

"Do you want to say something?" the doctor asked me.

"Doctor," I replied, "I want you to know that my future and that of my daughter, our lives are in your hands, the report you make is going to be very important. Please read these medical reports," I continued. "Look at the pictures. I have been asking for several months to see a neurologist, and my doctors and specialists have requested it several times as well."

"Please," I continued, "I need help."

He looked at me in a way I couldn't interpret. Maybe sad or maybe confused.

"Francy," he said, "do you know why you are here?"

"Yes," I replied. "But the information contained in those reports, plus all the evidence you can read from the doctors and specialists appointed by the insurance company, are the complete opposite to the reported information from the last specialist, Simon."

"I understand your position and I know that you work for the Workplace insurance company...", I continued.

"No," he interrupted, correcting me: "I am a consultant for the Workplace insurance ..."

"For this reason," I replied. "I know you will know what you should do after seeing those reports and analyzing all this." I appreciate your attention but remember that you have a responsibility to DUTY OF CARE that you acquired when you decided to become a doctor."

He looked at me and thanked me and the interpreter.

It took him three months to analyze the information.

I remember one night I talked with my daughter about finances because we no longer had money to pay the rent and I, with the frequent hospital stays, had not been able to work. Although my employer had voluntarily decided to give me 180 dollars a week for six months, this was a long time ago.

In addition, between what the Workplace insurance paid and the little that the employer gave me, only 20% of what I could earn in a week was covered, and on top of this, the employer only reported half of the hours that I actually worked there. This whole situation put us in a very difficult position, health-wise, psychologically, emotionally and economically speaking.

It was a hard day because, although my daughter is very strong, much stronger than I am, there was a moment when she came into the room and started crying.

Desperate, she said. "Mommy, what are we going to do?" she said. "We have no money, we can't pay the rent, what will happen to us?"

I sat her on my lap, took her in my arms and said: "I don't know, my love,

but everything will be okay."

That day we cried together. We were both scared. No one knew the reality

situation the two of us were in, but as I said before,

miracles always come at unexpected times.

The last thing I did when I woke up—if I got any sleep—was check my phone, but that day, for some reason, I picked it up and saw the email. I opened the report and cried, but this time from happiness.

They had sent the report from the specialist Julian. It said: "Miss Molina is not fit to return to work," mentioning all the medical reports and records that I had given him. "Francy requires further medical support, and it is urgent that she see a neurologist." Miss Molina's condition is complex and requires urgent investigation.

After 22 months of going around and asking for help, someone had the courage to do the right thing on behalf of the Workplace insurance. I couldn't believe it.

Then Laura, the advisor, wrote me a very politically correct email saying that at noon I would receive the payment transaction for the months they had stopped paying.

"My God, thank you!" I said to myself.

I called my daughter and showed her the email.

"See, my love?" I said. "God and the universe will always take care of us."

Nothing is Personal

With the new reports, the situation with the Workplace insurance became increasingly worse. If they hadn't wanted to give me the treatment before, they didn't want to give me the treatment now.

The owner of the company — who at first was very kind, promising heaven and earth, probably to avoid any legal claim by my side — also began to falter, while my daughter and I continued trying to survive the reality we were facing.

My health was getting worse every day, starting to fade away like foam in my hands. Every week I had more fainting spells, more injuries, memory loss, problems organizing my thoughts, problems with my Spanish, walking and moving, I wasn't sleeping and the pain was getting stronger and more relentless, along with painful migraines.

Still, I didn't give up and, believing that it was all in my head, I kept trying to go to work. I tried hard to deliver the results. I arrived at the office after spending entire days without sleep, with migraines and pain that made me faint.

In general, I was subjecting my body and mind to more damage, while at the office they began to notice that despite forcing myself to do my best, my health continued to worsen.

Then one day, I had a blackout where I lost my memory for a couple of days. While I was hospitalized, I was checked by several specialists, including a neurologist, who reported that I was suffering from severe brain damage, post-concussion, and possibly functional neurological disorder, or FND.

The doctors at the hospital ordered some specific tests to confirm the diagnosis and told me that I should be kept under observation for at least a week.

To my surprise, the workplace insurance denied the investigation again! I had no money or private insurance to cover the costs, since the private insurance would not cover it, because it was a work accident.

I was left without these tests, and the hospital staff released me without any problem.

My daughter, angry, confronted the doctor in charge that day.

"Don't you see how my mum is?" she said, crying with indignation at seeing the way I was being treated. "How can money be more important than a person's health? She needs help!"

To which the doctor cruelly responded: "This is not personal, this is a business."

I detested these words, unethical and meaningless, which are only a fatal way to destroy lives by justifying an infamous action in an inhuman capitalism lacking empathy".

The embarrassing thing is that I heard this every day

from people I thought were intelligent and humanitarian; the thing that makes me a little curious is to know if these same people would repeat this phrase or say the same nonsense if they were in a situation like mine or worse. Anyway, I think it would be a good psychological study of empathy, emotional intelligence and other behaviors.

Of course, for the person who says this cliché, it is nothing personal because it clearly does not affect the life of that person or the people he loves, and he cares very little about what happens to others.

In addition, the little phrase contains a small part of the ego telling you "I do not see you as a human being who deserves respect, care and support, but as an object that makes me money, and if you cannot give it to me, you can die." In short, and in addition to being unfair, it is a cowardly, unintelligent, egocentric and dirty phrase, more typical of a psychopath or sociopath.)

After my daughter finished interacting with the doctor, the nurses told us that we had to wait for a taxi and the taxi driver would pick us up from the waiting room.

When the taxi driver arrived, he took one look at the state I was in and furiously told the nurse that he thought I was going to pass out. "What are you trying to do to her? he growled, "I am not taking her in my taxi while she is so unwell".

Then the nurse, finally embarrassed by the situation, ran to get a wheelchair. I sat down, the nurse called for another taxi and on our way to meet it in another part of the hospital, we passed by some police officers.

My daughter told me to stay there, and she'd be right back. When she came back, she was crying inconsolably. I asked her "What happened, love?", and I hugged her.

She sobbed, "Mummy, I asked the police if I could sue the Workplace insurance company, but they told me it wasn't possible."

Surprised, I asked her, "Why do you want to sue them, my love?"

She replied, "Mummy, they're going to end up letting you die if we continue like this."

I hugged her while biting my lips to hide my sadness as I was breaking down inside seeing my daughter like that. To be honest, it was the first time I felt anger towards these people - the advisor, the manager and all their unscrupulous circle.

I realized the people of the Workplace insurance company could do whatever they wanted with me, but what these criminals, with a license to destroy lives in the eyes of many people, never understood was the damage they were doing to my daughter. I cannot describe these people as being any different from criminals.

They were destroying the life of a young girl who needed care and protection. They were violating her rights, and they had no compassion for her. They excused their behaviour based on laws that only supported their desired outcomes for the company. This is just unacceptable.

After that, at my meeting with the owner of the company I still worked for, he had the audacity to ask me for a "clean" medical certificate that would state that I had no health problems. This was obviously impossible for me to do, and he knew this.

He then told me I could no longer work for the company until I had the required "clean" medical certificate. In English one would say that he completely washed his hands of me. This left me with health problems on top of the other problems I already had.

"Please," I begged him. "I just need help with medical treatment. Maybe if you talk to the Workplace insurance company, they will authorize the tests and other treatment that is needed. That's all I need to recover and be able to come back to work as before." I was foolish to believe that he would care about us."

Then something happened that had never happened before with him. Tears started pouring down my cheeks, and just like the doctor at the hospital, he repeated the well-known phrase. "It's nothing personal; it's just business."

It was the last thing I heard from him, and I still remember it like it was yesterday. Coward. Maybe it was business for them, for us life had taken a 360-degree turn and it didn't stop. The saddest thing about this was that everything that was happening to me was the result of their negligence and lack of security for employees, not to mention the lies and information they were hiding about my attacker.

That day I came home and thought to myself: "My God! Everything is falling apart and I can't do anything! Indeed, the company removed me from my duties, a decision that has made everything worse than before".

My daughter and I dealt with the situation alone and in silence, trying to pretend that everything was fine, until one day, the bomb exploded.

Looking at everything that happened it is difficult to see all the damage that was there. Can you imagine being in a country and feeling afraid, intimidated and not having someone to ask for help? It is terrible, threatened, sad and hopeless

New Discoveries

It was 2022, around the time Australia, was hit by terrible floods. I was sitting in the living room of a friend's house having a Zoom telehealth appointment with my psychiatrist.

I tearfully told him, "No-one is listening and something is wrong with my health. I feel explosions in my head, as if I was hit very hard, I feel dizzy all the time, the headaches are overwhelming, and I randomly lose consciousness... that is not normal."

Then he looked at me in astonishment, I had never cried in front of him in 22 months. Then he said, "Francy, I am going to admit you to the clinic to monitor you and see what is happening. Organize who you are going to leave your daughter with and in three days I will call you to admit you to the clinic"

At first, the psychiatrist Erick thought I was depressed but got a huge surprise when the show at the hospital started. Nosebleeds, migraines, vomiting, loss of consciousness, blood pressure of 45 that did not go up with intervention, heart rate above 185 beats per second or more that did not go down with intervention and mobility that was getting worse.

During spells of unconsciousness, my blood pressure dropped to 40 or 45 and my heart rate, along with my breathing, slowed down alarmingly. Each fainting spell caused me to crash into things, such as sinks, toilets, showers and the floor. The crashes only aggravated my condition, my brain injuries, and more injuries throughout my body. Consequently, I have repeatedly injured my arms, legs, head, chest, and other parts of my body. The nose bleeds were constant, and the dizziness worsened.

The worst thing about this is that I never knew when I was going to pass out and I couldn't control it, which is complicated because it's extremely risky and possible to die in one of these episodes.

In one of the fainting episodes, the paramedics spent 35 minutes trying to bring me back to consciousness. I always feel bad for days after these episodes and they get worse each time. It's been a miracle that with more than 100 fainting episodes I've only caused damage to my hands or face, because when I fall I hit the floor or anything around me.

None of this is easy, I had one or two epileptic attacks, but I don't have epilepsy. For some reason that the doctors can't explain, it just happened.

During the fifteen days I was under observation, Elisa, the GP at the clinic, told Erik, the psychiatrist: "She doesn't have a mental problem that can be attributed to her condition, except for post-traumatic syndrome, depression and anxiety, which is reasonable with this woman's situation. She has post-concussion symptoms, severe brain injury, and everything shows that the issue is neurological. This must be investigated by a hospital with all the equipment for neurological investigation"

I remember I was asleep when I opened my eyes and saw Erik sitting there, watching me.

"Dear Francy," he said, "We are worried about your situation. I never thought you were this bad."

"I have been telling everyone this for months," I replied, frustrated.

"Yes, but you say it so calmly…"

I stared at him.

"I can't discharge you," he continued. "You're going to kill yourself in one of those blackouts, and I'm not going to take on that responsibility."

In the following days I had the worst fainting spell, I had ever had. Fortunately, it was in front of one of the nurses. That was when, worried, Erik called Elisa, the GP at the clinic, and told her: "We need to do something with Francy urgently."

She answered "I need to do comprehensive tests,"

One of the tests went wrong, and I was rushed to one of the hospitals for a more thorough checkup, but to my frustration, that day I was seen by a doctor who had a preconceived idea about people who were referred to by the psychiatric clinic. I don't know how to describe her… Let's just say that the mistreatment I suffered under her supposed care made me feel much more pain, covered me in bruises, and I tried to escape from the hospital and return to the clinic, sad and disappointed to see that there are people like her practicing medicine.

I called Andrés, my GP, and he called the hospital. However, there was not much he could do other than file a complaint and speak to the doctor concerned, asking why she had treated me that way.

The hospital called to justify the doctor's aggression, and everything was left in limbo.

(To be honest with you, I have been severely affected by racism, discrimination and stereotype in the Australian system during this whole process. I have witnessed how many people do wrong to other human beings, but no one says anything. This behaviour makes them complicit in a chain of disasters, the saddest thing is that they forget that it is another human being who feels and breathes just like them).

By this time, Erik, the psychiatrist, was worried. I had already been put in a wheelchair because my mobility had worsened, and I couldn't get out of bed unless one of the nurses monitored me and made sure I wasn't going to lose consciousness.

He sent a letter to the Workplace insurance company and Laura from the Workplace insurance company came out to say that she would not authorize my transfer to another more specialized hospital with the equipment needed to diagnose my condition.

This upset Erik. He wrote a letter explaining the reasons for his request. I was never able to read the letter, but I do know that it must have been very compelling as Laura from the insurance company responded within three minutes, authorizing my transfer to a hospital with the appropriate equipment to investigate my condition.

The conclusion of twenty-nine days of medical observation and testing was the following diagnosis. I have Traumatic brain injury, concussion, neurological functional disorder, psychological damage, post-traumatic stress syndrome, depression, panic and anxiety attacks. I also have the following physical injuries: involuntary tremors, loss of mobility, short and long-term memory loss, broken bones, hearing loss, headaches, constant dizziness and chronic pain. There is also the whole circus of symptoms that, to this day, we still do not know how to control - high and low blood pressure, high and low heart rate and low oxygenation.

The terrible thing about any accident is that you never know what the damage is until the car stops spinning, and it lands, if it ever lands.

For me, the diagnosis was just the beginning of the complicated reality that I would now have to accept and learn to live with.

On that day, October 13th at 6:45 pm, the person who once, danced, cried, smiled, and dreamed, and who arrived with her suitcase full of dreams to Australia would never be the same again.

The nightmare

Someone once said, "Ignorance is a gift," because once you know what you're in for, you don't know all the things you're going to face.

The day we got the final diagnosis was a scary day. The doctor told us that as a consequence of the Traumatic Brain Injury, I developed a Functional Neurologic Disorder. FND had no cure.

She explained to us that if this injury was not treated in time, I would probably end up reduced to living connected to machines that would help me perform certain basic functions of my body.

These are the things you never want to hear: That you might die—or, perhaps worse, be left in a vegetative state—and that you will be leaving your child alone, unprotected, unsupported, uncared for, and even with the great responsibility of caring for you, because you cannot do it for her, or even for yourself. Feeling, in that moment that there is no one to hear your prayers except God and universe.

I was scared. Not for myself, or for the pain, or for the path that would lead me to that moment. I was scared because I realized I might not get to see her, or my nieces grow up and leave my family and those I love alone. I was panicking that I hadn't done my job well as a mother, to leave her alone in a world that is very beautiful but can sometimes be cruel.

My 14-year-old daughter looked at me, frightened. I looked back at her, and our eyes filled with tears. Neither of us cried at the time, but it was clear that we were both frightened by the prospect the doctor was presenting to us. When I left the specialists consulting room, I could feel empathy with every person who is diagnosed with a rare disease and whose prognosis is hopeless. At the same time, I felt a great appreciation for life, for being alive and being part of the world.

We both held hands and cried. With certainty, at that moment, that it would happen, we said to each other: "We will get the treatment needed and everything will go back to normal,"

But this statement was very far from what would be the reality for us. Back in my hospital room, accepting that I needed help and accepting the disability diagnosis, cost me tears, hugging pillows while I screamed in pain and biting them so that no one could hear me, going into the bathroom and letting the shower water cover my tears so that no one could see them fall.

Humbly accepting that I was now dependent on a nurse to go to the bathroom to relieve myself and to call her when I wanted to leave the hospital room in my wheelchair. Losing my independence left me feeling trapped in my body, in my mind and in the room.

CHAPTER II

Life after diagnosis

What Does This Diagnosis Mean?

In this chapter I will give, from my humble knowledge, a brief explanation of what the diagnoses I was given are and what this means for me and for the people around me, not only in a purely functional way, but also from an emotional and social point of view, since the repercussions of this incident in my life are many and across many levels.

I must clarify that I am not an expert on these issues. I am not a neurologist, nor an expert on injuries. However, during my studies in psychology, I learned a little about how the brain works.

And over the past few years, thanks to my GP, my psychologist, and all the other experts who have been with me, as well as my having read and studied for a long time, after my diagnosis, books on neurology and on the functioning of the brain, to understand what was happening to me, I have been able to go into a lot of depth on this subject. I certainly believe that 'knowledge is power' and a valuable tool in situations like mine and other illnesses.

Furthermore, I believe that sometimes, beyond having titles, people who suffer from a disease like this or any other have a lot to contribute based on our experience. So, in a bold way and with my empirical experience in this situation, as a person affected by this disease, I will try to explain my understanding of what it is about, based on what I have lived through all these hours, days and nights, months and years. I must clarify that the experience will not be the same for everyone, but the symptoms in general will be similar.

Note: What is mentioned in this book is based only on my symptoms and my experience. It is important to recognize that Symptoms are different for each individual, depending on the individual circumstances.

Traumatic or Severe Brain Injury

Brain injury occurs when a blow, impact, or jolt to the head causes damage to the brain (or when a penetrating object such as a bullet or piece of bone enters the skull, but clearly not my case).

This can lead to bruising, tissue tears, bleeding, and other physical injuries to the brain, which can cause a coma, put you in a vegetative state, or even death, and can even lead to long-term complications such as physical, communication, or intellectual problems.

In my case, I have a severe brain injury, which has produced serious physical and psychological symptoms. I experience memory problems, headaches, migraines, permanent unbearable pain, dizziness and sometimes nose bleeds. It may also have caused problems with my balance.

With proper treatment, a person may recover from a severe brain injury.

Some treatments include physical rehabilitation therapies, occupational and cognitive neurology, speech therapy, psychology, psychiatry, psychiatric medications such as antidepressants, anticonvulsants, or anti-anxiety medications, as well as stimulants and muscle relaxants. In some cases, surgery may be required to repair fractures, remove damaged tissue, hematomas, or relieve pressure.

Post-Concussion

Concussion is basically a milder brain injury. Some of the symptoms, such as headache, dizziness, and problems with concentration and memory, can last longer than expected— weeks, months, or even years. This is known as post-concussion syndrome.

These symptoms usually go away over time, but because of all the hits I've taken (with the fainting spells), my symptoms are constant.

Post-Traumatic Stress Disorder (PTSD)

Post-traumatic stress disorder (PTSD) is a mental health condition that develops after experiencing or witnessing a particularly traumatic event. Many people develop this disorder after experiencing a life-threatening event, such as war, a natural disaster, an accident, or sexual assault, among other circumstances.

Typically, these types of situations generate fear and stress, which causes an increase in adrenaline that allows you to respond to the danger effectively. Typically, these effects return to normal when the danger is no longer present, but when you have PTSD, that stress and fear can persist over time, or they can appear and disappear suddenly at any time.

PTSD symptoms cannot always be controlled, and they can be triggered, especially when the unconscious responds to a stimulus that can revive the experience, without the person being able to understand what is happening. Not understanding PTSD can lead to erroneous comments and behaviors in the people around you that only generate more stress for the affected person. For this reason, it is important to understand that PTSD is a real condition and that the person who suffers from it has no responsibility or control over what causes it.

Symptoms of PTSD may begin right after the traumatic event, but sometimes they may not appear until years later. This usually causes the person to constantly relive the trauma in the form of flashbacks, recurring thoughts, or nightmares, particularly when you are in the presence of something that makes you relive it - even if it is just a temporary event or remotely - the situation, and again feel the fear, anguish and anxiety that it generated at the time of the event. This makes you constantly alert and aware of danger, making it very difficult for you to rest, sleep or concentrate on an activity.

In cases like mine, because of this, you start to avoid things, people or places that remind you of the event. This makes you lose interest and the desire to do things that you used to enjoy and makes it very difficult to create or maintain relationships with other people. This doesn't help the situation much, because you feel distanced from the people you love the most.

There is also a feeling of guilt or remorse. The person feels that they acted wrongly, or that you could have done something differently, and sometimes the person blames themselves for having done wrong. (And of course, having everyone telling you what you should have done in the situation does not help).

This affects your self-esteem, making you feel very bad about yourself, making it difficult for you to see the positive side of things and, of course, making your perspective on the future become very negative. This can even generate suicidal thoughts.

As you might imagine, all these symptoms cause considerable problems in social or work situations and in relationships. They can also interfere with your ability to do normal daily tasks. It is usually treated with therapy and medication, especially anti-depressants. It's really hard to describe, because it's so strange. One minute you're going about your normal life, and then all of a sudden you feel scared, and you don't know why.

It is clear that your rational mind tells you that nothing is happening, but your subconscious sends you other information, or when you have these flashes of the traumatic situation you had experienced, it simply takes you back to that moment and the sensation that you experienced, or when you cannot sleep because you are so afraid that, as soon as you close your eyes you wake up sweating and trembling with fear, disoriented or screaming.

How do you explain to someone that going to crowded places can set you off and you can possibly have a panic attack where you can't breathe and then you start to choke, and your body starts to shake without you being able to control it?

How do you explain to someone that you feel sad, that you lack interest, that you don't want to get up in the morning, that nothing matters to you and that everything is over for you because you don't know what is happening with your life? That you, no longer find meaning in the day or the night, that you are not interested in listening to or seeing anyone, that you would like the earth to swallow you up.

How do you explain to yourself that it is not your fault and that it is a process that must be healed like a broken bone, without feeling ashamed of yourself?

Functional Neurological Disorder (FND)

Functional neurological disorder (FND, as I will call it from now on) is a relatively new and little-known disease, which is still being studied by neurologists, in its early stages of research, as perhaps many diseases were in their early days. So, there are clearly contradictions between the different specialists, who with their big egos often make terrible mistakes with their patients (And, of course, I include myself on the list of guinea pigs).

What is FND?:

FND is a problem with the functioning of the brain and nervous system in which signals are not sent or received correctly.

What causes FND?:

The exact cause is unknown. Physical triggers or physical injuries have been suggested as possible risk factors for FND.

Diagnosis:

Diagnosis must be made from a detailed examination and the patient's medical history.

Symptoms:

A wide range and combination of symptoms may occur. Neurological disorders include mobility, speech, memory, fainting and many more.

Treatment:

Retraining the brain, unlearning abnormal and dysfunctional movement patterns, and relearning normal movement.

How can you help?

• **Education** about this rare disease is essential to provide support to the diagnosed person, not to fall into unfounded opinions that may affect the life of the person with the disease.

• **Support pets in Australia,** as in other countries, are used as support for some physical and psychological diagnoses. Several studies have shown that animals such as dogs and others can detect any abnormality in the person long before they feel bad, such as epilepsy and other illnesses.

• **Exercise and physical therapy:** depending on the person's health status, daily exercise or physical therapy can help improve the loss or deterioration of mobility or involuntary movements, muscle strength, among other physical and psychological benefits.

• **Hobbies:** in the midst of this complex situation, it is important that the person continues to carry out activities that motivate him or her to continue. Example: Cooking, listening to music, painting, going out of the house, movies, depending on the tastes of each person.

• **Get a support group:** if possible. Family support is essential for the diagnosed person. Maintaining relationships with friends is important.

This information has been collected from people who work with this new disease and who have an important track record researching and supporting patients with this diagnosis.

¡How I explain it and what I understand!

In general, FND is a disorder of the nervous system in which the brain stops sending and receiving information, from one or more parts of the body, correctly. An example of this is the muscles or senses, especially the parasympathetic and nervous systems. Basically, your brain connects with the nervous system to perform all kinds of activities. However, if this connection is broken or interfered with, there will be a kind of short circuit.

Symptoms of FND depend on the type of disorder, but generally affect movement or senses, such as the ability to walk, swallow, see, or hear. It can also cause pain, weakness, paralysis of the limbs, seizures, tremors, or jerking, as well as anxiety, depression, insomnia, or fatigue. All of these symptoms, while not life-threatening in themselves, do vary in severity from person to person, and can lead to serious complications in your functional performance, your ability to function in daily life, and your overall quality of life.

In my particular case, this disconnection of the brain

occurs in the parasympathetic system, which is the part of the nervous system that allows your body to regulate itself and all those things that you do every day to happen automatically without having to think about it: getting out of bed, going to the bathroom, running, walking, remembering, maintaining balance, among many others.

So, when you disconnect the nervous system, there starts to be a number of open windows that generate errors in your body and that is where the problem begins. Fainting, loss of mobility, nosebleeds, loss of sensitivity, migraines, dizziness, vomiting, vertigo, memory loss, loss of sleep... And in general, feeling like your body is starting to collapse.

It's a strange disease. One minute you're smiling, and five minutes later you're on the floor, unconscious, with pain that simply disables you. You're talking and suddenly you have brain fog as if you weren't even there. The hardest part of all this is the loss of mobility and memory. It's very hard for a person who is used to having an active, independent life to lose mobility and freedom.

FND has no known cause and in many cases, no one can

identify what triggers the symptoms, but sometimes symptoms may appear suddenly after a stressful event, a brain injury, or after physical trauma.

FND is not related to structural damage to the brain (such as when there is a stroke, infection or injury), but to the way it functions. Depending on the case, FND is treated with Neurology, Cognitive Therapy, Physical Therapy, Psychotherapy and Occupational Therapy, Speech Therapy and other treatments, but, as I have discovered, if it is not treated in time, it can gradually become an increasingly severe and disabling condition.

In short, as you can see, what I currently have is a cocktail of ailments/conditions that when combined generate a condition that is sometimes merely annoying and sometimes totally disabling. This is how I explain it and what I understand my illness

The Medical Odyssey

Living with FND is living with a disease that many know exists, but no one knows how to treat, and when you mention it to most medical specialists, most of them just want to throw the hot ball and run away.

After having had so many MRIs and brain scans, the medical team decided that it was becoming too dangerous for me to continue, as I could develop cancer. So, it was decided they wouldn't be doing anymore unless it was an absolute emergency. For the time being, they would hospitalize me and see how I reacted after each loss of consciousness.

I realize that there are many health professionals who do not have the time or interest to investigate new conditions such as FND. However, I have been very fortunate, since Andrés, my GP, Dayana, the psychologist, Violeta, Manuel, Lucia, among other experts and all the people who have supported me during this process, have taken the time and made the effort to delved deeper into the topic of FND to guide me along a long path, but with hope. This has made an immense difference in my life, since with their support and advice it is easier for me to understand and face this new situation.

For me, everything changed during my therapy with Dayana, my psychologist. At first, it was very difficult for me to be honest about what was happening to me and what I felt. I firmly believed that I was going crazy, as I once explained to her. To which she replied, "I don't think so. You have something called post-traumatic stress disorder (PTSD), which is normal in people who have suffered a traumatic event. However, that should be diagnosed by a psychiatrist."

A few days later, I was referred to Erik, my psychiatrist. Thanks to both of them, I was able to understand and learn more about the condition. I only told them, "I can't sleep because of the pain." And yes, I was in terrible pain. What I did not tell them was that I was having horrible nightmares and was waking up sweating and afraid.

Erik did his job thoroughly in determining that the

problem was neurological and not psychological, which the insurance company would have preferred, after refusing to let me see a neurologist for months. A detailed study and careful observation by nurses and a GP, a physiotherapist and the psychiatrist determined with medical tests that there was something that did not correspond to a purely psychological diagnosis.

Thanks to them I finally saw the neurologist, as well as a cardiologist, a physio, a rehabilitation doctor and a GP. They all have experience with FND. They confirmed that I had a neurological, not only a psychological, problem. They advised the Workplace insurance company of their findings and the prescribed treatment I would need, but the Workplace insurance company said they would never provide it.

When I go to a neurologist who doesn't know how to explain FDN or how to handle it. It's possible that you'll end up like people who had epilepsy problems 100 years ago, ending up in a mental health facility. Of course, if you speak to a professional who knows about this rare disease and has experience in these cases, they will shed light and explain a little of what this consists of.

After everything that has happened, I am of the opinion that there are two types of professionals: Some who do serious, respectful, ethical and professional work, but there are others like Simon, who have major conflicts of interest and whose job is to support the system regardless of the consequences for the affected person.

Private doctors, fortunately are more professional and are bound by their oath about the care they provide to any patient that they treat in a fair and responsible way, see the patient regularly and are more independently and supporting when giving suggestions to the insurer, because they are not answering that Workplace insurance, which allows them to do their work objectively with their patients.

As much as we want to say that doctors and patients do not mix for ethical protocol, let us not forget that we are human and that there will always be some emotion in our actions. Taking care of our patients; being empathetic, compassionate, respectful and objective, for me is professionalism, and there is nothing unethical about it.

UNETHICAL is harming another human being knowingly, for money or for personal interests. And this is my journey in the Medical Odyssey.

How do I feel about my diagnosis?

The journey with this disease is cruel and hard: I wake up every day at 5 or 6 in the morning, starting the day with 3 or 4 hours of sleep, tired and in pain. I spend entire days in the hospital, fainting almost every week. I usually greet the people around me and answer the everyday question of "How are you?" with a smile and saying that I am fine, even though the truth is that 60% of the time I am exhausted and in pain.

I survive the hard days, and the good days too. I smile a lot and treat others with love and respect because that is who I am at my core. I talk to God - my God and the universe - and thank him for the love and compassion he has shown me, for taking care of us, my family, my friends, and other people who care for me, for giving me courage every morning, because only he knows the reality of this situation. I keep quiet most of the time so as not to worry others.

It always seems like everything is fine and, to tell the truth, this is my way of dealing with this reality.

It is important to highlight that when we have a toothache we are not ashamed to admit it, when we have a headache we go to the doctor without fear or prejudice, but if something is wrong inside us in our mind or feelings then for some inexplicable reason we write in red and capital letters "She has mental problems", "She is crazy".

And the fact is that the aspect of mental health or disabilities is seriously punished in certain cultures, countries, religions, communities. I had someone I love and respect very much going through complex mental health issues, and I was not judgmental at all with her or some else. Even having studied psychology and worked with people in some vulnerable situations, I never realized what this really meant until I experienced it myself. It was then that I realized I had my own stigmas.

My stigma was not in looking down on other people or

being prejudiced under any circumstances. My stigma was in recognizing that I needed help. The hardest blow to my pride (and to my ego, because that is what it is, after all) was when I was hospitalized for 29 days. Then it was impossible to pretend that I was okay with someone monitoring me 24 hours a day.

So, while prejudices and taboos pass through certain people who are stable, people who are going through a moment of loneliness, confusion, sadness, afraid, uncertainty or hopelessness, feel ashamed and hide as if they have done something wrong.

So I started to notice how is it possible that it is believed that the appearance of the exterior is more important than our psychological part, that it takes so lightly and with prejudice a situation where the person clearly needs more than ever a hug, a support, a kiss, a warm word, a simple "You will be okay and we are here for you"?

The hardest thing for me was to accept that I needed help. We have been raised in a social, religious and family environment where it is not well seen that we are vulnerable, where it is difficult for us to ask for support from others. For some strange reason we believe that being vulnerable is being weak, and this is what happened to me. For months I was fighting with a physical, emotional, mental illness, economic hardship, struggling not to let my daughter down. However, when someone said to me how are you, I had no qualms about saying good (GOOD?) REALLY? I was going straight to the cliff and I still did not want to accept it.

Because the truth that I don't tell anyone is that extreme situations (or tragedies, as they are sometimes called) put me in dark places, locked rooms, hopeless moments that make me fall to the ground and don't let me get up. My days become endless and painful, lonely and empty.

Along with the wheelchair and the disability diagnosis, I began to feel locked in my body, imprisoned, not knowing how to handle these mixed feelings of sadness, frustration... I also realized that it wasn't just feeling locked up within myself: it was also losing my freedom, that I loved so much, and that I took for granted. Going for a walk, running, swimming, driving, dancing, going to the gym, going out with my daughter and with my friends, but especially - and the hardest to overcome - losing my job.

Inside me, my soul is torn apart and constantly screams for freedom. I am locked in this place, in my thoughts, and inside this prison where there is so much loneliness, so much pain, sadness, silence and sometimes anger. This prison that is my body and mind is the place where I am trapped at this moment in my life. A dark, sad, disconnected, scary, intimidating place. It is a place where loneliness settles and thoughts taunt me, mixed with the "Why can't I end all this?"

With all this, mental health begins to play a fundamental role. It is like a **TOXIC** relationship that I still cannot close, overcome, heal, understand, but I keep trying to get out of it. I miss my life more than anything, not saying what I feel does not mean that I do not feel it or that I do not live it day by day: I live with fear, with sadness. Trying every day to move forward no matter what happens around me.

Living in these circumstances is something I have not accepted, even after all these months. I find it hard to understand when I went from running and being healthy to being in a wheelchair, from having fun on weekends with my daughter and my friends to being in an emergency room almost every week.

I still can't accept that I need a diary to remember almost everything, I find it hard to get someone to help me bathe. It breaks my heart not to be able to be a mother, sister, daughter, aunt, friend, worker and not to be able to be self-sufficient to do things like drive. I find it hard to get up and see the wheelchair. I fight with it in my imagination. I find it hard to be alone and see myself in the mirror and not recognize myself.

Doing my therapies and putting on a strong face while the pain is killing me and the heart monitor shows 189 beats per second before my fainting spells, because I refuse (and will always refuse) to believe that this is going to be my future. I have learned from nurses, books, doctors, specialists to have more compassion for myself if I want to continue living.

To accept that the wheelchair was going to be my companion for a while, but never my best friend. However, and although some said that I would be much worse by this time, the struggle, the constancy, the perseverance plus the help of many people and specialists has made it possible for me to still move, to speak, to eat, to still have a small window of what is called quality of life, even when at times it may seem so small. I have faith. I believe without seeing.

I have hope, love, passion to move forward and one day be able to help others with everything I have learned in this process.

And so, in the middle of the prison, a light always comes on that says that everything will be okay. I close my eyes and I see myself walking, even running, without fainting and without the pain that I feel right now.

That light or window in my internal prison is what gives me the courage to get up and continue another day on days like today. It's my life, it's my spirit, it's my soul, it's my body, it's my brain and only the universe, God and I can control it; I am convinced that we can overcome it and learn to handle this.

It is the best decision, of course, without stopping to close my eyes, seeing myself dancing salsa and enjoying with my daughter, being free, smiling. I still dream, I still trust that this will pass and that what I will keep as a lesson will be more valuable than the pain and suffering that this situation has brought to our lives.

Of course, after everything I have experienced, my perspective has changed. I am convinced that it is important that we can recognize and seek help in the most inclement moments, a good helping hand can help us make things more bearable. For now, when I look in the mirror, I can accept that this is me, now, and that this is what is happening to me.

I do not know if this situation is forever or is simply a temporary walk in this wheelchair.

Social Stigma

Along with illness comes indifference, intolerance, ignorance, and unfounded comments. Because of my current condition, I have learned how complex it is to be called disabled, to be looked at with reproach or disapproval or ignored by others, and all that this involves.

From my point of view, many people put anyone with a disability in a separate box. This allows them to act as if nothing is happening and continue with their life and their daily routine, without thinking that we feel alone, isolated, scared and rejected in these situations.

My world has changed since I was 33 years old. I have seen everything, but I am still waiting to see the best of humanity: That feeling of love and brotherhood that we all carry inside as part of every human being.

My experience includes being kicked out of taxis and Ubers because the driver refused to provide service to a person in my condition. That, added to the fact that I use a wheelchair, has made me feel discriminated against and destitute. It is appalling to see how some people treat you when they see you in a wheelchair. They look at you with disapproval, they reach over you disrespectfully, it is their social stigma that influences their behavior, as such they take up your space as if you did not exist, they ignore you... To the point I reflect and wonder; what is happening in today's society?

There are so many stories to tell that I might never finish, but I assure you that some have been simply heartbreaking and traumatic. It is incredibly ignorant to speak and give an opinion about something when the person doesn't know the whole truth; when someone is not living or feeling what the person diagnosed feels.

It is pretentious and violates people like me; who are going through this situation. The illness alone is painful. It breaks my spirit, it disables me, and if we add to this the ignorance plus the lack of tolerance of others, in a situation like this, everything becomes even more complicated.

Getting used to the looks of rejection from many people who ignorantly judge me and feeling like an insignificant grain of sand, hurt me at first. I did not want to go out. Then I said to myself: Who are these people that I do not know and who do not care about my life? Why am I giving them power over me? With each look of rejection, with each incoherent comment of mockery and ridicule, I gathered billions of grains of sand with which I built a castle where I pray for them, because they do not know what it is to be in this circumstance or what it feels like. With all my love in the world I hope that they never go through a situation like this, or anything similar.

On the other hand, there are people and organizations that are tolerant and respectful. These are my favourites: Children who look at me with curiosity. Some say hello, some smile at me, others simply show empathy and respect. Just like some adults who are surprised to see me in a wheelchair. One of the most beautiful experiences I have had is this little boy in the Shopping Centre: I was driving my wheelchair; he came up to me and said "Give me five" and put his little hand on my hand. At first, I thought he was making fun of me, but then he looked me in the eyes and said, "You are a wonder woman. You are and never forget it." Then he "high fived" me, smiled at me, and left. It has been one of the most beautiful experiences mixed with wonderful feelings that have given me joy and hope.

Another beautiful experience happened while we were at the beach. When crossing the pedestrian walkway, we saw a father with his beautiful little girl. She was no more than 5 years old. They looked at me, then both greeted us with a beautiful smile. I greeted them and smiled back at them. After a moment I saw the little girl get into their car and look for something. I looked back at the sea. Then I felt a small hand on my shoulder. It was her. In her little hands she was holding a beautiful drawing full of colour and joy. My eyes filled with tears. I hugged her and thanked her.

The drawing has been everywhere with me since that day two and a half years ago. Sometimes, when I have a hard day, I look at the painting, and it makes me feel happy and peaceful.

Situations like these show me that there is still hope. That there are many wonderful people in this world, including my community on Instagram who, when I disappear for a few days, write to me and ask "How are you? Are you okay?"

These are people I didn't know, but for them I still existed, and they undoubtedly felt love, mercy, and compassion for another human being regardless of whether they knew them or not. In the end, people like me who are diagnosed with rare and disabling diseases do not infect or kill anyone. Many like me just want to move on.

There are many people diagnosed with physical and psychological health problems, for example autism, depression, post-traumatic stress, among many other diagnoses or injuries. However, if you look at some of them, they have been geniuses and humanitarians like Frida Kahlo, Albert Einstein, Stephen Hawking, Audrey Hepburn, Steve Jobs among many others who, according to society, were not "normal". They are a source of inspiration, courage, bravery, intelligence, kindness and evolution for humanity.

My Angel

The illness not only changed my life but also affected my daughter's life too. At 13 years old, she had to take care of her mother and deal with hospitals, doctors, police, lawyers, detectives and insurance. Something completely unfair for her.

A year after the incident, my daughter was so sad, depressed, disappointed and afraid because the person who had offered her stability could no longer give it to her. Instead, she was now the one who carried a huge responsibility and was suffering the impact of this situation while her world seemed to crumble beneath her feet.

Despite the circumstances, she has remained strong, she has carried out her studies alone, being decorated on several occasions for her dedication, performance and results.

At a young age, she got a job contributing to the household expenses, without anyone asking her to do so. It is admirable how wise and dedicated she is with everything she sets out to do and she has done everything on her own these past four years, making me feel very proud of her.

Looking after me in my current condition is not easy, even for an adult. There are days when I suffer from chronic fatigue or intense pain that does not allow me to get up; during the night I usually cannot sleep because I do not feel well; I regularly have fainting spells... And she is there, taking care of me as a mother would do with her child: she takes care of me, feeds me, comforts me, and although tired she still goes to study or work.

It's easy for others to comment on the effect of my condition on my daughter's life, when they only see our situation from afar, especially when I'm fine. But if there is anyone who knows the reality of the situation, it's her.

I don't need to tell her what kind of day I am having, because she has got to know me so well during ALL these months. She has been and continues to be my nurse, friend, confidant, daughter, without pay, providing care with a lot of love and patience, even when deep down she is exhausted and sad.

And of course, I can dress up this whole situation by

saying that it will probably help her in the future. Of course, it is true that this will make her stronger and of course that is something that will help her in life, but I also know that the scars will remain with her for a lifetime; I don't think it is fair that she should carry such a burden.

As a mother, I know that when we love our children, we never want them to go through a situation like this. Certainly, I feel pain and broken hearted for my daughter, and I would give anything to relieve her of this burden that she has had to carry.

I would give my life, if it were necessary, for her to be the least affected by this situation. It would be foolish to say that I am satisfied that this will make her stronger, because I am sure that if you are a mother or father and you are reading this book, you would not want to see your 13-year-old son or daughter go through a situation like this? I am sure that many will agree, so why should I feel lighter about the fact that this is how it is and this is how I need to accept it will continue to be.

But the reality is that I carry the illness, and she carries the three of us. The illness, me and herself. She not only took responsibility for her mother, but she also had to find herself in the difficult place and position that an immigrant finds themself in when we talk about legal issues, rights and health.

She, without saying much, can truly empathize with many immigrants who have been treated unfairly in vulnerable circumstances.

And you won't see her as a victim crying or telling everyone why her mum is in a wheelchair, or why I have fainted. You will see her putting on a brave face in every situation and trying to prevent someone else from coming into our lives, fighting to take care of what remains of our lives and realities; strong as only she can be; sometimes smiling, other times quiet and expectantly observing what is happening and what others say.

For me it is a miracle and a blessing that she is by my side, because without a doubt she has been my weapon and my shield in this war, even when I am wounded and without strength.

She is empathetic, quiet, introverted and observant. Since the incident her life has changed, but she has adapted in the best way possible to express her own feelings and has not fallen into inappropriate behavior. It has not been easy, but she has achieved it with bravery, dedication and a lot of courage, because if this type of situation destabilizes an adult, imagine what can happen to a teenager.

After all these months, I can see in her a lot of courage, a lot of love, a lot of empathy, but also a lot of pain and sadness. I hope that one day, not too far away, I can heal the wounds and help her heal the sadness that this situation has left and continues to leave in her, because, although difficult circumstances promote values and create stronger people for a better society, I consider that it is something that she should never have had to face.

I was unable to protect her as I should have and that hurts and disappoints me, because I was the one who brought her to this place with the promise of a better future and, although in some ways it has been, she has had to pay a very high price for it. I love her smiles and her cuteness. She lights up my dark days and celebrates the bright ones. I understand that this is not something we can change with a magic wand, but thanks to her, dealing with this situation has become easier.

The path

I think the biggest barrier to overcoming an illness like this, is 'oneself', and that is that I live in fear of being judged, labeled, rejected and even isolated for expressing what I feel; and because of that, I lock myself in and am afraid of opening up to other people, as if this was all my fault.

Breaking these beliefs and being able to say "I don't care what others think" was the greatest achievement in this stage of grief. It is not easy to sit back and see how my life changes have occurred, and for one second not be traumatized, after being almost beaten to death, without adding the pressure of all the other circumstances.

It is not easy to get up every morning after many fainting spells and several blows; to depend on others for almost everything. It is not easy to understand and accept how there can be so much evil in the world until you sit face to face with the people from the insurance company, the lawyers and other people who are only there to bring you down. It is then that I ask myself: What in the world is going on? Not understanding why, because I am an immigrant in this country, I am treated like garbage by many organizations such as the Workplace insurance company, among others, making me feel that I am simply worthless.

This leads me to bigger questions: "What am I in this world for? What is my purpose on earth? Which path should I follow?". There is the first path: staying in bed taking opioids all the time to keep the pain down, taking medication for PTSD and depression and staying there, numbed by the effect of the drugs on my system and my brain.

There is, of course, the path of hatred towards everyone, which could be justified, and, in many cases, I find perfectly understandable that a person could take. Finally, there is the path of getting up and being thankful because I can still see my daughter's beautiful face, I can still hear my family on a call. Because there are beautiful people who come into my life every day, and because there are more difficult situations that I see every day in other people, this is why I can only be thankful, smile and carry on.

Each one chooses our own path, and this does not mean that one is better than the other, because as I have mentioned before, we are all different people. We have dreams, thoughts, joys, sorrows, traumas, unhealed and infected wounds. Each one of us has our own world.

Not all of us are cured by taking traditional medicine, not all of us are cured by taking alternative medicine, not all of us are cured by meditating, not all of us are cured by whipping ourselves.

Each person has her or his own way of dealing with things and healing his or her wounds. It can take, perhaps years, perhaps a lifetime like for war veterans, who after going to combat and seeing everything they see, going through everything they go through, can sometimes never heal.

However, in my personal experience I believe that whatever path we wish to take, be it psychology, psychiatry, coaching, consulting, confession, meditation, spiritual retreats, writing, hypnosis, working with energies, chakras, etc. All paths are valid as long as that path helps us heal and does not harm anyone else.

But first you must take the first step, which is to admit to yourself that you need help and then seek it where you feel most comfortable, never in addiction or alcohol. Without a doubt, these can make you sink to the point where you may not find a way to return, and then getting out of there will be almost impossible.

Like me, there are thousands of people who hide, out of fear of what others will say or out of fear of rejection. Our mental health is as much our personal responsibility as our physical health. Everyone has difficulties; some wounds are deeper and more infected, but it is up to you to decide how far you allow your mind to take you. Remember that our brain is as wonderful at creating as it is at destroying.

Don't be silent. Find someone good that you can trust without feeling ashamed. Find your own way to be happy in your own way, not in the socially imposed way, or in the way that others dictate to you, but always remember to promote respect and tolerance for others.

Depression, anxiety, traumatic stress disorder and panic attacks are things that can happen to everyone. These situations are just as important as the physical part that we pay more attention to. Surprisingly, your mind, your spirituality and energy are the fundamental bases of your physical well-being, even when some beliefs say something different.

CHAPTER III

After the Diagnosis

Coming Back to Home

Coming home after being hospitalized for 29 days, feeling heartbroken from being away from my daughter, who was so young, I decided to ask the doctor to let me leave the hospital.

He was not happy with my request, and told me that I clearly needed help 24/7, and that the fainting spells placed me at a very high risk of losing my life, adding to this, I needed physical therapy every day, if I wanted to stop the degeneration that was causing the different injuries and other diagnoses.

However, that day, through tears, I told him:

"Doctor, I have a 14-year-old girl alone, without her mother. We have no family or support here. We know very few people. She needs her mother."

When I got back to the apartment, I was surprised by an unexpected visit: Doña Luz is a woman who came to this country several years ago with many dreams, including helping the Latin community in Australia and the vulnerable people in Colombia. Doña Luz is a strong, religious, loving, brave woman who runs a restaurant from which she helps anyone who is facing difficulties. We had met years before the assault, and she had little by little seen me blossom.

We began a friendship based on mutual respect and honesty where we shared things from daily life.

When she saw me, she was surprised. She was one of the very few people who knew about the incident.

We hadn't told anyone else, except perhaps a couple of very close people.

When she saw me, I noticed a little sadness in her eyes, which are always warm and bright, like a party. In her blood and in her roots is that joy, cordiality and love that identifies Latinos and my people.

"My Francy," she told me, "You need help. Let me help you."

"Doña Luz," I replied. "I don't like to talk about my

problems. I've never felt comfortable with this."

"My Francy," she continued wisely, "there are very good people out there";

"You will find people who will help you and who will give you a hand so that you can get out of this situation. YOU MUST open yourself up so that you can rise again."

She is a woman of faith and very devout. Her love for God has allowed her to see life in a thousand colors and become a testimony of life as she herself would say, and how can I say that this is so.

"You need someone to take care of you right now," she continued. "Someone who will be there and accompany you when your daughter is not here." "Have you thought about bringing over someone from your family?" she asked me.

"Yes, Mrs. Luz," I said. "My brother, but right now I do not have the funds to pay the expenses."

She looked at me and said, "No. You need your mother. You need the care that only a mother can give her children, with love and patience." I looked at her and realized that she was completely serious.

"But I can't do that right now," I replied.

"I'm going to help you make that happen," she assured me.

I looked at her again and tears welled up in my eyes. My mom, in Australia? That was something that seemed completely out of reach for me at that moment, but deep down I knew it wasn't impossible for her.

She left my apartment leaving me ajiaco soup, my favorite food, and at about 4:00 PM she sent me a message telling me that she needed to talk that same night. By the time we spoke, she had already spoken with some acquaintances of hers who have an agency here, who were going to help her for free with everything she needed to issue the visa that would allow me to bring my mom to Australia.

Mrs. Luz decided to have a fundraising event at her restaurant where she would serve ajiaco soup and all the money raised would be used to pay for my mom's airfare to Australia.

"My Francy," she said, "Please make a short video where you invite people to the ajiaco."

I looked at her and said to myself: "Should I record a video?" Don't take this the wrong way, but I was terrified.

For those who don't know me, I am a very calm person and you will almost always see me happy, smiling.

I like talking to people and I am, as some people would say in my country, "very hi person" (because I never refuse to greet anyone). However, despite that, I have always been afraid of social media, the camera, and photos. All of this despite the fact that for a long time, as mentioned in **the first book, THE PHOENIX Part I** (the beginning of my life), there were periods in my life when I helped vulnerable communities in my country and had to talk in public several times. But it was at this point in my life that I understood the great fear I had of being exposed and of being seen as vulnerable.

Until that day I had always fought my battles with the help of God and the universe. I had never asked another person for help. At least not on this scale. Eventually I did it. I recorded the video, sent it to her, and within a few minutes she had already posted and shared it everywhere.

Before the event, Mrs. Luz asked me for the account, then she put my bank details with the price of the ajiaco in the messages. How surprised I was when I checked the account balance and saw that I had $1,800 after having only $100? At the end of the event, the cost of my mother's tickets had been collected in full, It was simply amazing, magical and absolutely incredible!

The day of the event was magical, comforting, and exciting. It filled me with energy, joy, hope, and showed me the best of

people.

Mr. Ricardo and his wife arrived with rice pudding to sell as a dessert and donate to the cause. They, along with Jorge, who has an agency, had called more people through their social networks. They volunteered to take orders, wait on tables, and take calls. I, who had decided to go to the event despite the health issues, was at the cash register receiving money from the event.

The event was attended by people from all over: many of them wanted to talk to me and others looked at me curiously; all the faces had something in common. You could see the love and empathy they felt for my situation.

It was a wonderful day. I felt so much love and happiness, today I still remember the great feeling from that day. Thanks to everyone for that amazing day.

Among the many issues that arose during the visa process for my mother, there was the one-off presenting the results of her medical examinations and the fingerprints. During the time my mother worked for many years in the florist, they used chemicals that destroy fingerprints in the long term.

At that time she was supposed to have her fingerprints taken, but only a few were successful. I remember being in the hospital, half drugged after fainting and hurting myself quite badly, when she called me almost crying and said:

"Honey, I'm sorry, they can't take my fingerprints."

"Mother," I said. "May it be what God wants." We had already done everything possible.

So I told one of the people who was helping with the visa about this situation to see what advice he could give us. Then a miracle happened again. I don't know if it was thanks to the intervention of the people who were carrying out the process, but something surprising happened.

I remember the day and how I felt, when I got a message that said: "Your mother's visa was approved." I was almost awake again. I cried on the gurney in the emergency room, because I never thought that this would happen this way, and although the circumstances that brought her to Australia were not what I would have wished for, God, the universe, and the community made this possible.

The day came to meet my mother at the airport. I had had an episode a few days earlier. My face was black from the fall, but I was excited and put on makeup as best I could. My daughter, Mrs. Luz, and I went to look for my mum.

When I saw her come out of the airport door, my heart stopped. I looked at her and saw that she was more beautiful than ever. She looked at me, and although she is a strong woman, in her eyes I could see the sadness of finding her daughter in a wheelchair. We hugged each other, we kissed each other, I gave her flowers. My mother thanked Mrs. Luz and the entire community for allowing me the privilege of having her by my side at one of the most decisive moments in this story.

These months were confronting for both of us: I still didn't know how to ask for help, and she didn't know what to do to help me. She felt alone, sad, frustrated, since she couldn't speak the language and, therefore, she couldn't express her frustration to other people at seeing what was happening to her daughter.

However, I have no doubt that bringing her to Australia was the best decision. Having her by my side gave me strength and allowed me to recharge my batteries. There was someone who took care of my daughter and me, as only a MOTHER knows how to do things for her children and grandchildren. With love, with care, with courage and with compassion.

Mother, I am so sorry for the reason why your heart is sad today. I have always thought that you deserve the best in the world, but sometimes life puts us in situations that we cannot control. Thank you, mother, for all your love, sleepless nights, tears and smiles. I love you.

With my mother here, it was impossible to continue hiding what was happening from my family. I began to see how each one of them fell with me in every faint, suffered with me every fall and lived with me every moment, with a frustration greater than I could feel, but without losing hope that "La flaca" would recover.

When my brother found out about my condition, he also put together money with great effort, doing everything possible to travel to Australia. He arrived a month before my mother had to return home. For my brother, taking care of me was very hard. There were nights when I knew he was sad, even though he thought I didn't notice, but in the end, he faced the whole situation with love and warmth, always acting like a great human being.

Every time he picked me up from the ground, I remembered the time he was a baby, and I held him in my arms for the first time, so beautiful, small and defenseless. Now he was the one who carried me and took care of me when his work and study allowed it.

Being an immigrant in any country is not easy. For those of us who have walked this path alone, we know that you have to shoulder the burden to make things work out. My baby brother was with me for a year and then returned to the family.

Goodbyes are not my thing, and I think they are not my families either. We know that we will meet again one day, and then my mother, sisters, brother, nieces, daughter and brothers-in-law will sit at a table again to share a meal. I will cook for them to show them my love as I did when we were together.

Distance does not end the love I have for them. I know that sometimes we have our differences, but I know that this will not separate us, because we are family and because love is the foundation of our relationship. There is nothing that together we cannot achieve; each one, thanking God or the universe, we trust that everything will be fine for everyone.

The fact is that family is a group of people that we do not choose. However, they are the ones with whom we face the good and the bad circumstances, because we are blood, because what happens to one of us affects us all. There is nothing more valuable than family and when we are all united and pull the rope together, nothing is impossible.

For now, I have beautiful memories of my mother and brother visiting me, taking me to the beach, making me laugh, keeping me company when they could, listening to me when I needed to talk. I am left with the joy and pride of knowing that my brother has matured into a wonderful man, a man who can overcome anything and who has an admirable character.

Workplace Insurance

After the diagnosis came the next phase of my nightmare. Until that day the Insurance Company had initially not wanted to accept my condition despite the reports from the different specialists. When they finally accepted my traumatic brain injury, they took the position that the condition was not necessarily related to the attack and in order to approve any kind of treatment, we had to prove that the Neurological disorder had been a consequence of the incident.

Thus, the agreement with the Insurance Company was that, if after my hospitalization, which lasted 29 days, the neurologist determined that what was happening to me was a result of the attack, they would pay for the medical treatment until there was either a complete recovery or at least some improvement.

A month after my hospitalization ended, the neurological report came out confirming that the traumatic brain injury and all the other injuries were a direct result of the attack. The suggested medical treatment was that I be treated by a group of specialists which included a physiotherapist, a neurologist, and a pain specialist, among many other specialists.

However, even after receiving the report, the Insurance Company shamelessly wrote me an email saying that they would not cover the treatment, claiming that the condition has no cure. The only thing they approved was for me to have a course for chronic pain management. Without further explanation, as usual, they closed the case.

I started attending this course, but with the frequent and dangerous fainting spells that occurred while I was in class, the person who led the group contacted me to tell me that he was very sorry, but it was very risky for me and them to have me in the course. Then the company that ran the course wrote a letter to the Insurance Company sharing what had happened and explaining how dangerous the fainting episodes are. But as always, the Insurance Company ignored the opinion of the specialists.

Without argument, I can say that the Insurance Company has played a fundamental role in the danger and unnecessary stress I have been exposed to. They are cruel people who have no empathy and who do not care about destroying people. They have no compassion for the person, their families or the circumstances.

They are ruthless, they play dirty, and they laugh in your face. Also, as I mentioned before, they are racist. They discriminate against you and take advantage of your circumstances to put you down. Of course, some will tell me that this is their job. That insurance is a business which receives money to cover a risk that has only a low probability of occurring and that it must ensure that, as far as possible, it does not have to respond in the eventuality that this situation occurs. It must look for all the obstacles to ensure that it does not have to pay out and that the money stays in the pockets of the investors rather than paying for the treatment of the affected person.

My question is: Who has the heart, ethics, values and principles to harm the lives of other people to take care of their investors' money? Because that is the fight. Money that only enriches some within a capitalist and unequal system.

The funniest thing about all this is that I have never wanted the money for itself, but to allow me to have dignified, continuous and responsible treatment that would allow me to return to work and perhaps be the person I was before this traumatic and dirty situation.

The worst thing and what surprises me the most is the number of people who, out of fear, just keep quiet. There are a large number of accomplices involved in the irresponsible handling of cases. On the list of people that work for the Workplace Insurance you will find GP's, specialists, neurologists, physiotherapists, psychologists, psychiatrists, and of course the crows. This is what I call the lawyers.

I would also include the State itself and do not forget the employer. Since my assault I have met several people who, out of fear, do not report the management of their case by their Workplace Insurance and who, even when they are in poor health, say they prefer to keep the problem to themselves rather than face these monsters.

Crows

Certainly, and for many reasons, I think that this country is an excellent place for many things. However, there are other things that remain the same or worse than where I come from. One of them is the issue of lawyers. My history with them has been one of the most complex, difficult and inhuman things I have ever experienced, because here paying a lawyer costs 10 times more than in my country, and if you don't have the money to privately pay for their services you have to organize yourself to get something called "If you don't win, you don't pay." I will see at the end of this process how true this is.

Basically, this was the legal model that I was able to afford. However, to be honest, at least for the first 14 months I resisted the idea of starting a legal process. I was able to make this choice because, at the time, my employer said that they would be supporting us during my recovery and the owner assured me that he would not abandon us, until I was stable and making money again. (Obviously, because he knew the huge mistake he had made, but I will explain this later with more details).

The belief that I would be able to return to work one day, even though at this time our financial situation was very difficult, kept me from taking legal action. I must add that many people – including my colleagues – told me to do it, but I was aware that these legal processes are complex and if you don't understand the language and terminology... Oh my God!

I approached a Legal Firm to find answers to the many questions I had about my condition and circumstance before I was prepared to commit myself to the legal process. At the first meeting, the gentleman who attended to me was very polite and promised me heaven and earth. He also promised to translate the documents so that I could sign them in peace. However, I had not made up my mind to go ahead with the legal process. Rather I wanted to find out what was involved and if this was the path, I wanted to take to achieve my treatment goals. I asked the gentleman many questions with my treatment and recovery, the only thing on my mind.

However, in the mind of the Workplace insurance, they were finishing me off no matter what. In the mind of my employer "If it doesn't work for me, then fuck it" and in the mind of the lawyers, "We have to get all the milk out of this cow" (Or, better yet, I am something like a blank cheque to the bearer for them).

With desperation and following the advice of many people, including my colleagues, who told me:

"Francy, your employers are going to leave you hanging and they don't care about you or your daughter. You need a lawyer now,"

plus the serious level of abuse from Workplace Insurance, the constant deterioration of my health, my worries about the welfare of my daughter and also our financial situation, I decided to return to the Law Firm...

When I arrived there after 4 months, I was surprised

when I saw the firm had prepared a contract, at least 30 pages long, and completely in English, ready for me to sign.

I asked the person in charge for the translation, to which this person replied.

"I have to talk to my boss." telling me later that day, "We are sorry, but we cannot translate the contract. You have to sign it like this."

Under all this pressure and trusting this person (Not much in the boss to be honest: There was something about him that I did not trust), I signed it.

Their promise was that they were going to do everything possible so that I could have decent, timely treatment and other lies only to get me to sign the papers. And then I saw that months went by, and they did nothing.

The few emails that were sent to the insurance company asking for something were more because they were requested by me not upon the initiative of the Firm In reality, they had not started to investigate the case. Then it got to the point where I said: "These people are billing and not doing anything, so I better move on."

When I cancelled the contract with the Firm, I already owed them approximately $11,000 for making calls, some emails and that was it. They did not secure treatment for me.

The second Legal Firm was recommended by two people. One of them later told me that she had made a mistake recommending that law firm, and indeed I agreed: The day the lawyer called me, I was not sure about starting the process with them; however, when I spoke to him, he seemed like a sensible person. I would say: "He is a good person, but he works for someone not so good."

The issue with these new lawyers was clear from the beginning. Once I had told them about my condition and explained: "If I did not manage to get the treatment on time, my health would deteriorate, so it was urgent that the treatment was approved and that they represent me before the Workplace insurance company efficiently." Again, they committed themselves, but these ones turned out to be even worse than the first ones.

They divided the case into three stages. The first was their intervention between Workplace Insurance and me, according to them, for money to handle treatment and other issues. The second, if that did not work, my case had to be filed for reconciliation. They explained what would happen and how they were going to represent me. The last part was - if I'm not mistaken - that we went to court.

The truth is that the experience with these second lawyers was even more terrible, stressful and disconcerting than with the first ones. I remember that they let the case go to the last stage of the Workplace Insurance's jury, assuring me and believing that, because I was sick, I was also stupid.

This only brought me more problems, including realizing that someone from my community, who had helped me raise money to bring my mother to Australia, had held direct conversations with the owner of the Legal Firm, breaking the minimum ethical practices of privacy and confidentiality of the client. However, here is a secret that no one tells you: the law only works for the benefit of the legal profession, not for the client.

What does it mean for the affected person when the case goes to the Workplace Insurance jury? When a claim goes to the jury, which is made up of three people hired by the insurance company, who claim not to work for the insurance company (they define themselves as advisors to the Workplace insurance , which for me it is the same with a different name) whose purpose is to close the case. Once this happens, there will be no more coverage of medical treatment and no support from Workplace Insurance.

The case is closed and that's it, leaving the claimant unprotected. To this end they made an offer; however, in my case what they offered was not even enough for six months of treatment, but I had no choice but to accept it.

Absurdly, what this second Legal Firm wanted was to close the case with Workplace Insurance not caring that my health had worsened rapidly. The only thing they wanted was to get money from the first stage and continue milking me in the second and third stages.

I decided to end my contract with this second Legal Firm. With my signature, I received a bill for another few thousand dollars for emails, calls and on top of that, for breaking the confidentiality clause! Nice ones! No?

Several things to reflect on from my point of view of this situation: The first is that there are really no ethics on the part of some lawyers who, seeing the damage and pain that is being caused to the client, are only interested in getting the greatest possible benefit to fill their pockets with money.

Second, something disgusting is that the person has to practically hand them all the information needed for the case, ready for them to do something, otherwise the affected person is screwed. The third is that they really seem like bullies, waiting for the last breath of the affected person, when they come out like crows to eat everything they can.

A legal process is quite complicated, especially when you are sick, in constant pain, when language is a barrier, when you don't know the laws well. If we add to this the fact that these people, who are paid to fight for your rights, are helping you sink slowly for their own benefit... What can I say? It is macabre, unethical and unprofessional.

Many, a time I have heard people say that the lawyers and the Workplace Insurance are just doing their job. In my opinion, this is a dirty and baseless justification.

I am now with a third Legal Firm. This firm came to me because one of the people who was taking care of me told me: "You can't be left without lawyers, especially at this stage and with your state of health." I remember when Francisco arrived at the apartment and my daughter spoke to him. He said that it was not his place to judge anyone, but that the previous lawyers had not done things as they should have.

He assured us that he would help us. It was clear that payment for the treatment would no longer come from

Workplace Insurance, since the previous Legal Firm had let the process go to the insurer's jury. Francisco advised me to accept the money that the insurer was offering me when they closed the case, indicating to me that, if I did not take it, it would probably be 3 or 4 more years without receiving any money. He committed to starting a new legal process.

Again, the reality I have had to live with has been disappointing. Promises and more promises. They did not investigate in time, I gave them the most of the information they have, they had no idea that there was a legal process against the person who had attacked me until I informed them and, like the others, they continue to play the macabre game of seeing how much my health deteriorates to see how much money they will get.

Unfortunately, although my experience with this third Legal firm is as bad as the first two, I have decided that I cannot change the system so I must stay with them. It would cost me too much mental and physical effort and, as I have said before, my body, my mind and my spirit are no longer able to take it.

At this moment I can only trust in God and the universe for everything to turn out well. Disappointing, frustrating, painful and outrageous, but apparently that is how things work and there is not much I can do about it.

And if on this side it is not pleasant, on the other it is confronting and quite intimidating to face the lawyers from the defence. They are mean-spirited people, who would do anything to destroy you in any way imaginable in order to line their pockets at the end of the case. Their job is, without a doubt, to destroy the plaintiff no matter how they turn your life upside down, even if it has nothing to do with the incident.

They don't play fair and enjoy intimidating people. Really when you see a case on TV it's not over-acted, the defendant's lawyers are just as gruesome as you see them. I constantly tell my psychologist - they are ruthless towards me. They use psychological intimidation (which is a well-known form of torture in the different media, especially in wars or with prisoners).

When they can't end your life, they will make your world the worst place for you and everyone around you. But many say that it is their job and that it is ethical, and I will leave them with their own opinions, but those who have gone through processes like mine know what I am talking about. I am sure that there are many people who, like me, have reached the point of trying to take their own lives because of the same pressure that they exert on each victim that comes into their hands.

There are certainly values that should not be lost. One of them is **ETHICS.** Seeing people as human beings and not as numbers. Justifying the damage that these companies and professionals do to others is something unbelievable and heartbreaking. And it is all to capitalize and fill their pockets by using another person's complicated circumstances.

I don't think it is necessary to go through such an absurd, sad and painful situation to realize that good is good and bad is bad. Let's stop embellishing things with clichés and unjustified justifications.

On the Edge of the Abyss

Even before I was diagnosed, things at home were already pretty difficult. I was out of work, couldn't pay for food or rent, and I couldn't afford the medical treatment I needed. Add to this, of course, the constant pain, the depression, the uncertainty of knocking on doors and experts not knowing what to do, the fact that the system limits your rehabilitation services, the exhaustion of fighting with Workplace Insurance to get decent treatment, and all the responsibilities that life entails - because one thing is certain: The assault happened, but life didn't stop.

After the diagnosis, everything got worse. It was clear that in order to recover and continue with my normal life I needed a lot of specialists. However, the treatment is expensive. According to the general opinion of the experts, I will need it for life. Of course, this is impossible for me in my current state. Apart from the financial challenges, too much time has passed for this to be an easy process.

The fact that I have missed so much of the initial medical treatment has left me with both physical and mental challenges.

The issue of rent also became much more critical. I had already fallen behind on several payments and without money to cover the monthly rent, it was clear that I would eventually have to vacate the place where I was living with my daughter.

Worse still, the visa with which I had arrived in Australia was about to expire, and without it my stay in this country was complicated, at least legally. (Which, you can imagine, made the situation much more complex when I was in the middle of a legal battle, and trying to obtain medical treatment).

Keep in mind that for me, returning to my country in this condition was not an option. There are no professionals there who can handle a case like mine, and I currently do not have a health plan that would allow me to cover a treatment like the one I need. In addition, I was sure that any dispute I had at that time with Workplace Insurance would have to be handled remotely from the other side of the world, and that would only mean that, in less than a minute, my case would be closed and archived.

The Workplace Insurance knew that me being left without a visa was an ideal situation for them, since being in the country illegally, they would have an excellent excuse to send me away and get rid of me, or to corner me so that I would agree to whatever they were offering.

In fact, several people who have experienced similar situations have told me that many times Workplace Insurance takes care of putting people in an extreme situation, to pressure them and get them to the point where anything, no matter how small, seems enough.

Around that time, someone told me to write a letter to the Prime Minister and the Minister of Health, telling them about my situation, asking for help with my treatment or with my situation with the Workplace Insurance. Many people and some MPs helped me with the letter, to the point where I got more than 20,000 signatures, but after I sent it... Silence. Nobody answered me.

So, with the pressure of having nothing for my daughter and myself to eat, I had to go to several donation places. It was a complex situation, but the important thing was that my daughter and I then had something to eat.

In the midst of these circumstances, there was always an angel who reached out to help me. A charity foundation took us in and helped us find a new home where we could be at peace with more reasonable payments.

The response from the Minister of Health came almost a year after I had sent the letter. It was an official, cold and impersonal letter, in which they told me that they understood my situation but there was nothing they could do

Caregivers, Angels and Friends

Along with all the difficulties and trials that came with this new stage of our lives, people and organizations came along and reached out to us from their hearts and did the best they could to help with many of the situations we have faced. From that very beginning, the paramedics joined in writing reports to their managers, telling them about the complexity of our situation and my health, telling them that my daughter and I were alone, that we had no permanent residency, that I couldn't work, and that I needed constant care before one of the fainting spells ended fatally.

More angels began to appear, sending letters to different non-profit organizations and other private companies asking for help for us, trying to obtain funds for my care.

Little by little, more companies began to arrive. One of these was Blue Care, which at first said that it could not provide me with the service because I was not an Australian citizen.

However, after speaking with the manager for 50 minutes, she called me the next day at 6am and said, "I don't know how, but we are going to get at least a few hours a week to help you with your care and with the household chores that you cannot do."

It was a very beautiful moment because, even though those who should have responded but did not, like the Workplace Insurance and my employers, new people who had nothing to do with the incident came to open new doors.

With the change that the assault meant, another implication came. I was not able to work as much as I wanted to, as my employer, the company responsible, wouldn't give me the opportunity. My health was very fragile and no matter how hard I tried, my body, my mind and my essence were collapsing.

That was when the non-profit organizations that worked to keep us afloat arrived. All the organizations have been excellent. However, since Amparo's arrival, many things have changed for us, the support we have from them has been transformative.

Amparo transforms lives by filling the entire family with hope, understanding, love and strength. The organization is made up of a group of people who love others. Their purpose is to help people with disabilities and their families, especially those of us who are immigrants and whose first language is not English. They make you feel like family. It is beautiful to find something like that, especially in such critical times like these.

The caregivers who have been with me have played a fundamental role in the process of my recovery. People like Donna, Hilda, Jessica, Marta, Laura, Angela, the list of people is too long to mention here. They have offered me their love and care, reminding me that everything will pass at some point, and some of them have been with me for a long time, being pillars of love, commitment and care for me.

Working as a caregiver is not easy. You are accessing the

person's privacy, and depending on the values that each one has, it can be a very delicate subject - something that I have experienced. And the same goes for family. Opening the doors of our home to a new person is never easy, especially with all our personal issues.

I share more with them than with friends. In the midst of day-to-day life, it is common for us to exchange personal things, such as about their cultures, their beliefs, their lives. Many of them left their countries like me with the hope of making a better life. I see in each of them the great value of leaving everything behind to come to a new country with the dream of improving the quality of life for their loved ones.

Many of them are single mothers and others have husbands. Single mothers show me the enormous love that I identify with, where giving everything for their children is an act of pure heart.

Some of them, as happened to me, still have their children in their countries of birth and their greatest desire is to bring them here one day. Others already have them here; however, they struggle with the difficult dilemma of being a single mother, paying for a student visa and covering the costs of their sons or daughters' school or kindergarten.

In short, being a mother in such conditions is a matter of courage, perseverance, love, patience and a huge effort that is only possible because of the immense unconditional love for our children.

Some of them are also grateful to be by my side, and they tell me that I am an example of strength and persistence amid the storm. I have very fond memories of all the people who have cared for me.

I remember those who, like Angela, have been with me for a year and who have always offered me love, respect and care. A person of total trust, who understands both languages perfectly, knowing what happened and seeing what we lived through day to day, only learned to love us more.

Liz is a wonderful woman who came into my life thanks

to another non-profit organization: She literally became my defender, caregiver, protector and confidant. Knowing all the information about the case, she always uses it to help me and protect us. At the time, when we almost ended up without a place to live, it was she who managed to get us a safe place.

She has fought for our physical, psychological, emotional and economic well-being and also for our rights. She is a brave woman with values and principles. Professional, persistent, determined and her respect for others is admirable. It has taught me and shown me that even though sometimes people are not how we think, there will always be people we can trust.

Liz became my role model, because, thanks to her dedication, effort, courage and charisma, she has given me back the hope and energy to want to continue working to protect and help others.

Hilda: A tender, humble and noble woman who has filled

my rainy days with smiles. A woman who is respectful even though I see her as a friend rather than a caregiver. She never takes advantage of my situation and, on the contrary, does everything possible to support me on the most difficult days.

Defining each person is a complex and almost impossible job, because with each one of them my perception of life, friendship, limits and trust has changed.

Of course, just as I have found wonderfully caring people, I have also found indifferent people. They have taught me that sometimes trusting them so much can be counterproductive, since they do not always know how to use the information they have in their hands.

It is not easy when sometimes people do not understand that this work is a work of love, respect, responsibility, care and privacy. They witness things that no one else sees and if they are not responsible, they end up being more of a hindrance than a help. Fortunately, this has been the exception rather than the rule.

Without a doubt, and although obtaining this service has been a challenge, I am grateful because thanks to their daily work our life is easier to bear, especially when my strength and spirits decline.

Another thing that has undoubtedly allowed me to continue in a more positive way and with a broader perspective, believing that despite what happens everything will be fine, is being able to count on the support of organizations like Ronald McDonald House, Romero center, Sherwood Community center, Victim Assist and Henderson Centre.

I think that being able to see the situations of other people and the reality that each one faces makes me understand that I am not the only one who is in a process of constant change.

Some of the stories that I have heard in different places have inspired me, because they are unique stories of heroes and heroines. Children and adults, who inspire real superheroes, who show me that nothing is impossible. When it occurs to me that my situation is complex, sometimes I realize that it is not like that.

These organizations were founded to help people in a variety of circumstances in which they find themselves, offering a helping hand when it is needed most.

Jonathan is my inspiration, especially after my life changed. I met him 7 years ago when I was volunteering at Ronald McDonald House. From the moment I first met him I admired him for his strength, intelligence and humility.

After what happened to me, I looked for him again to ask him to allow me to support Ronald McDonald House on a voluntary basis once more. Jonathan, along with Bec had no qualms about opening the doors of their organization to allow me to continue.

A month later, Angie took over at Ronald McDonald House and came into my life. Angie is an intelligent, kind, and noble woman. In these two years of being involved with the organization again, I have had major health setbacks.

However, neither Bec nor Angie hesitated to support me so that I can move forward, always leaving the doors open and hoping that everything goes well for us. In general, all the organization's staff are kind, which is nice. I don't work for them, I only support them in small activities, but being around them has generated confidence and self-assurance.

Tria has been another blessing. It's nice to be around her, to talk about what happened, without feeling afraid of being judged and with the assurance that she will have my back when I need it.

We don't talk much but when we have been in legal processes that are confronting, she is very supportive and caring. However, her extensive experience working with people who have gone through traumatic situations means that she has the perfect knowledge of knowing when it is necessary to stop. She protects me and gives me encouragement plus emotional and psychological support. Walking with her by my side on the two occasions we have been in legal processes has given me peace, security and courage.

Each of these people and organizations deserves an entire chapter, as they are places of hope, support and rebirth.

El Detective

Throughout this process I have met people with ethics and a broad sense of justice, who have helped and supported me selflessly.

People like the police officer who decided not to let my case close without justice. When I had to go back to the station to give more information about my case, most of the information had disappeared as if by magic. She, quite moved to see what had happened, decided to reopen the case so that a formal investigation could be carried out into what happened that night.

I gave her a new written testimony, telling her everything that had happened and the consequences of the attack, along with medical reports, photos, and examinations of what was happening. Then, I remember that, while I was in a car garage accompanying one of my friends, she called me.

"Francy:", she told me. "Your case will not be closed. A detective will contact you and will do a detailed investigation and get evidence along with testimonies that will later be presented to the court. I wish you good luck and hope this helps you and your daughter in some way."

Sure enough, the detective contacted me, interviewed me, and I'm pretty sure he followed up to see if what I was saying was true. After months of hard work, and with many difficulties, this brave young man collected all the information needed to get my case to court.

He even had to travel to Tasmania to find one of the main witnesses from that night, since the person had moved there and was not answering emails or calls. Then, one day, the detective came to see me and said:

"Your case is not going to go down as if nothing had happened,"

It was as if he had given me his word. He asked for my signature and told me that, although this person did not want to show his face, they had already located him and that he was going to look for him.

I remember quite well the day he came to notify me that a legal process was going to be initiated in court. I was hospitalized, my face was swollen, and my eyes were black. I watched from my bed the treatment being given to another patient. My tears started to fall again. I closed the curtain so that no one would see me crying, and when I pulled it back again, I saw the detective standing in front of me with the final document for the arrest warrant for my attacker. He looked at me, moved by my black face and the tears that were rolling down my face, then he said,

"I told you things are not going to be left unfinished."

I quickly wiped my eyes. He asked me to sign a final document and said that he wished me and my daughter all the best. That was the start of the legal process.

The Hour of Truth

It's been 39 months since the assault, and I am currently simultaneously involved in two legal proceedings. The first case is to prove that my employers are responsible for the medical treatment associated with my condition that was caused by the attack while in their employ, or failing that, that Workplace Insurance comes out to represent my employers.

The second case involves the State carrying out a legal process against the person who attacked me.

Justice here works in a similar way to that of the country where I come from. If the person has mental problems, they are not imprisoned in a jail. I prefer not to give an opinion on whether it is right or wrong. However, what I do know is that leaving this person without the care and supervision of a professional is a TIME BOMB... and as an example I have what happened in Sydney at the beginning of 2024, when a person entered the shopping center and with a knife began to attack the people he found in his path. 6 lives were lost.

The person had a complex mental health diagnosis and was apparently from Queensland, having arrived in Sydney just a month prior to this incident.

The truth is that this process ended up in the mental court, since the person has mental problems and cannot be prosecuted in the usual way, as would be done with a person without mental problems. So, the court has asked me to keep an eye on the prosecution case against the Bondi perpetrator to inform myself of how this process works.

A few days ago, I received a notice from my lawyer asking me to help him with some documents to continue with the legal process. What a nasty surprise when I read these documents and found that they contained the investigation of the day of my attack, with testimonies from three different people, information that had never been revealed to me, with the excuse of protecting me psychologically. However, things must move forward, so I had to read these documents.

The first document I opened was the testimony of the cowardly and greedy owner of the company. Clearly, the guy had no idea what had happened that day and it is logical. He was not there. However, to protect his empire it is easier for him to lie in a sworn statement than to face the consequences of his negligence and irresponsibility.

Given this, the first thing I asked myself is: What is going through the head of a person like this, who, in order to protect money, goes over the dignity, well-being, health and respect of another human being? WHERE DID THE VALUES GO, IF HE STILL HAS ANY?

The truth is that this corroborates for me that I have told many people who generally do not listen, and that is that we are nothing more than a money-making and profit-making machine for the company (for any company we work for).

Most of them are not interested in people or in the quality of life of their employees.

In fact, many business owners do not care if you live or die, if the company is exempt from any blame. For this reason, I tell you, it is important to always take care of yourself and think of yourself before the company.

The second "testimony" was from the employee of the place, who seemed to me to be more honest and sensible than the owner of the company. He stated that on the day I was working there were approximately 72 residents receiving care at the care home. They had to be cared for by the supervisor on duty, fed by the food assistant and provided with care by the members of the care home team. In this case the supervisor, the manager from 7 am to 5 pm and perhaps a caregiver for someone independent. At times there was only one supervisor looking after all 72 residents.

According to this person, they do a study of each resident they admit, and some of the residents were people with a very serious criminal history such as murder, rape, pedophilia among other serious illnesses and extreme situations. He also pointed out that it was not the first time that my attacker had assaulted someone and that a similar incident had occurred at another time and in another place.

Which left me speechless. My employer never, either during the internships, nor during the training, nor during the team meetings, informed us of the level of complexity of some of the residents' conditions, nor did they prepare us for high-risk situations. For me it is evident that the employers hid, eliminated and concealed fundamental information necessary for our most basic protection.

Thus, putting at risk the other residents, myself, the other supervisors plus other people like students and possible caregivers. The most serious thing is that they continue doing it as if this were the most normal thing in the world.

One of the workers at the organization said that he had

found out about my attack the same day it had happened, and he mentioned that it was not my fault and that he was very sorry for the situation my daughter and I were going through. He highlighted several points that to me are logical and just common sense, but as we say where I come from, common sense is the least common of the senses.

The next "testimony" was the person who trained me. He only said that I was a good worker and that I took care of the residents in a respectful and responsible manner.

I did not finish reading the document, as it is very confronting. However, my conclusion is that the organization is responsible for what happened, as they should have informed me of the mental health status of each patient and had more security in place, especially when they were housing potentially dangerous patients.

They are obliged to offer employees a safe place where they can perform their role without fear of these types of situations happening. This is simply a complete act of negligence that I have no excuse for anywhere.

The second thing is that it is obvious that if some of the people who are there have complex criminal histories, they should be treated appropriately and not as if nothing happened.

A few days later I had to attend the mental court. The summons said that the victim's attendance was not necessary. However, it was clear to me that there are things that must be faced to close cycles.

My intention to attend this appointment was reported to my doctor, my psychologist and my psychiatrist. One of them told me that it did not seem like a good idea, since my post-traumatic stress was still unstable. However, I consider myself lucky, because despite that, they supported me.

The session took place a couple of weeks later. To be honest, and since this is not a book about superheroes, but about people who live and feel, the night before the hearing I could not sleep at all. Even so, I got out of bed early, and the caregiver helped me get ready for the appointment.

At the appointed time I arrived at the hearing, together with the lawyer and the social worker who was handling my case, my personal caregiver and Liz, who has become my trusted friend. I must admit that it was a rather complicated moment, given that I felt overwhelmed by fear, sadness and frustration.

When we entered the room, they were talking about another case. Then the judge called the person who attacked me. He had not arrived, but his lawyer was there, who curiously began to make fun of me, or at least that is how three of the four people who were there that day felt. At first, I thought it was just my mind playing tricks on me, but then my caregiver confirmed that it had happened several times. I don't know what happened.

I feel that his behaviour was very disrespectful towards me.

When the session started, my attacker still hadn't appeared in court, and he wasn't answering his phone either. The judge said she wouldn't start until the person being charged appeared. She then asked his lawyer for his whereabouts, but he had no idea where his client was, or at least that's what he said. In the end they called a place, and he answered. To be honest, the person's voice didn't convince me, but it did convince the judge.

Initially they read the charges to him over the phone. It was in court that I found out that the person who attacked me had a very complicated mental diagnosis, antisocial behavior, among other complex diagnoses. Additionally, the same year he attacked me, he had attacked other people.

Finally, I got the answer to some of the questions I always asked myself about the attack, and that I had always been very curious about. One of them was the reason why he stopped his attack. Why hadn't he just continued beating me to death? Now I know why he stopped. During the attack, he injured himself quite badly as well.

More things were said in court; however, I didn't understand everything. The irrational thing about this issue is that the employers continue as if nothing had happened. During the discharge of charges, it was also mentioned that he had threatened some people, both before and after my assault.

In the end, I don't feel angry with this person who clearly could have finished me off if he hadn't broken bones in his hand. What frustrated and saddened me the most in the end is that my employers knew that he was unstable that day and, instead of placing him under observation, they left him without care as if nothing was abnormal.

CHAPTER IV

Final Reflections

Losses from a distance

During these 40 months I have been so engrossed in trying to survive my own war that I sometimes forget that the people I love are borrowed, and the truth is that I cannot simply assume that all those who love me, will still be there when I recover.

During this time, I have lost acquaintances, family, friends, my dog and, with sadness in my soul, I have had to recognize that I will never see them again. All losses in our lives involve a grieving process, this applies to all different situations such as losing a job, ending a relationship, bankruptcy, illnesses, among many others that according to some websites such as Medical News Today develop in seven phases that go more or less like this.

1. Shock: This stage usually involves uncertainty about the news.

2. Denial: This stage may involve rejection or other feelings about the news.

3. Anger: This stage may include feelings of rage directed at different people or institutions.

4. Bargaining: This stage, where one seeks to calm the pain left by the loss, may also present other feelings such as guilt.

5. Depression: This stage involves feelings such as sadness, loneliness, emptiness and loss of motivation to carry out daily tasks.

6. Testing: This stage involves trying to find ways to heal and alleviate the pain caused by the loss.

7. Acceptance: This stage does not mean that the person has healed, it only means that the person recognizes the new reality and accepts that they must continue with their life.

All the previous phases are difficult and painful. However, they are a fundamental part of the grieving process. It is important to note that if you go through any loss, whatever it may be, it is advisable to seek support.

Always try to say goodbye. Even when you are far away, you can say goodbye even if it is only by cell phone. Then you realize that there will never be another opportunity to hug the person or pet and thank them for all the love, care and company they offered you in this life. This is one of the moments when I understood that nothing belongs to us and that valuing the existence of others in our lives is a fundamental part, since nothing is guaranteed forever.

In memory of Olga Sepulveda (2021), Jonathan (2022), Pooh (2023), Irene Sepulveda (22-02-2025)

To be continued

As I write the end of this book, there are many things that have not yet been resolved. I am still waiting for everything to flow in a positive way for everyone involved in this story.

However, I want to share with you what this journey has left me with up to this day. It is not an easy situation and sometimes I get lost among my fears, nostalgia and despair. However, when I look back I can see how by a miracle and the love of others I have managed to move forward. All the obstacles that have appeared in my life have always come with a solution that seems like something fallen from the sky as a miracle.

As I mentioned before, I am not a religious person, but I do consider myself a spiritual person. I have faith, even though I cannot see or explain what is happening around me. Firsthand and as a faithful witness, I can say that, even though this situation is a constant cycle of falling, reflecting, and getting back up, I feel blessed.

And the love I have been exposed to in this situation from family, friends, organizations, and even people I don't know, such as doctors and health professionals, has been incredible and unconditional.

I know that I am in a continuous process of growth. Spiritual, emotional, healing wounds that were there and that arose along the way, learning to love myself more, to be more compassionate with myself and with the world around me.

Sometimes we cannot see the good in the circumstances that life gives us. At the moment of the storm, our eyes close and then we spin without stopping, allowing fear to take over our emotions and thoughts, throwing us into the deepest depths in the middle of a hole with no way out. However, when we allow our eyes to open a little after having fallen, we will find a ray of light that shows us where to start again.

The only way to overcome a complex situation like this is to be able to be thankful for all the good that has happened during the storm. Simple things like just opening my eyes in the morning, seeing my beautiful daughter's face, hearing and seeing my family on the phone, loving my friends and pets, being thankful for the roof over my head and the plate of food I have on the table.

Being honest, I am aware that, even without having many material things, I am a billionaire, because I have more valuable things that money can't buy. Those things that make my life meaningful and that make me get up every day, like in this moment of reflection where I bare my soul to share with you what has happened.

Many things remain to be closed and I know that in due time it will be so. Something I have learned is that timing is not something I control and that things come when they should. Patience is a virtue that is difficult to develop, but in times like these it is an invaluable treasure if you want to hold on to life.

This book is a tribute to people with physical and mental disabilities.

I am aware that I will never be the same person I was before this happened. However, I know that this version will be better than the previous one, even though I still don't know if I will be able to control my illness.

With each minute of my journey and with this new condition, I have learned that there is nothing more valuable than life and health; that money is only a resource that helps; however, unfortunately society ensures that money is everything and health takes a backseat.

As Steve Jobs said in one of his interviews, "I am the richest person in the world, but my money cannot pay someone to take care of this disease for me," This, for me, is an example that money is only something material that fades away when compared to the greatest truths and priorities such as health, love and others.

I had to live it to be able to understand it better. If before I felt love and great empathy for people who were going through complex situations, today I know that I am part of them and I know what it is like to be on this side of the road. This experience has put me in a different place, where I do not see the world the same way and where I am aware that this is only the beginning of this new journey for me.

Thanks to all of you who have accompanied me in this The Phoenix Rising. When the time dictates again, I will take my computer and write how this story ends.

With love, respect and admiration from me to all of you.

FAB

ACKNOWLEDGEMENTS

This stage of my life has shown me my true friends. Sometimes it is difficult because I am no longer the same as before, which makes it a challenge to maintain relationships with the people I knew before going through this situation. However, there are several people who stand out for being there with love and respect, taking care of me, despite the distance and remoteness of some of them.

Here I am going to take a few lines to thank these wonderful people:

Carolyn:

Memoirs of a Friend and Mentor.

At the time I met Carolyn, I was going through one of my existential crisis. I remember the first time I spoke to her. It was a sunny day. I was at the koala sanctuary, sitting waiting for a hot chocolate and carrot cake.

Liz had come looking for me, suspecting I was in the midst of an existential crisis, and Liz was right, I was. When I spoke to Liz, I told her I didn't quite understand what was happening with our lives and my physical health, which, along with the pain, was causing me to become extremely depressed. While I was talking, Liz looked at me, and I watched the birds fluttering among the trees near the river.

Then Liz told me she had a surprise for me. She told me she had spoken with Carolyn and asked if Carolyn could volunteer for some online classes. Carolyn happily told her she was interested. Carolyn has been an English teacher many years.

Carolyn is a very kind, smart, dedicated, and committed person to her students. Our classes began then. During one of our conversations, I told her about my book project, to which she delightedly replied that she would support me in the translation, editing, and proofreading of the English version.

That day, the excitement was overwhelming. Without

knowing it, Carolyn had given me another reason not to give up and not to disappoint her and the others.

For months, we worked together, almost every week, we met online for two hours to bring THE PHOENIX RISING Part II to life so I could share it and deliver it to readers.

Carolyn is an intelligent, patient, professional, and responsible woman, always supporting me in moments when I doubted whether what I had written would be good enough, giving me courage and confidence in the same way she taught me her language. She is a wonderful grandmother, mother, mentor and friend.

Dear Carolyn, although we haven't shared much, I feel honoured to have shared nearly a year of lessons, ideas, adventures, and the ability to trust you. Without a doubt, we didn't just work on a book together; we shared intimate moments on a level only an author and their editor can. THE PHOENIX RISING is written, but you helped me give it new life and make it a book that will undoubtedly reach thousands of hearts by giving me the opportunity to tell our story in English.

With love and admiration from your apprentice to my mentor and friend.

Ilse:

Friend, what can we say about this love that exists between the two of us? You have been with me for 17 years. You have seen me go through all the changes in my life. We studied psychology together, we went out partying, we celebrated our joys and defeats.

You are a person I admire a lot, but, above all, I admire you for how strong, loving, loyal and good a human being you are. You always think of people and help everyone you can. You are a wonderful daughter, sister, aunt, and a friend like no other. You have shown me your love so many times in a thousand ways. No matter how far away you are, from there you are always sending me the best energies and cheering me on so that, as in so many other situations, I can kick this one out of the park too. Thank you for being so unconditional and beautiful. I love you, my beautiful friend.

Ricardo:

You are light in my dark days. I love you as a friend and I certainly admire you as a person. You are loyal and, like the song, almost the perfect man. I want you to know that I feel great gratitude for everything you have done for me, for my daughter and for my family. Although far away, you have always shown me that you are a person with immense values and principles. Thank you for being in my life and for taking care of me so many times. I love you.

Enrique:

My dear Enrique: A friendship of more than 15 years has shown me that you are an unconditional friend, always encouraging me to keep going, listening in times of change, always confident that I will succeed somehow.

I miss you very much and I am immensely grateful for your help in editing and supporting me while I wrote these books. Without you I don't think any of this would have been possible

Paola:

My beautiful Pao: I am happy to have met you and to have you on my path. Although our personalities are very different, we have built a very beautiful friendship. You, my Pao, have been there in the hardest moments of this process, and I have been fortunate because, despite the situation, you have never looked for an excuse but have always come and supported me wherever I am, with a hug, with your love, understanding and prayers. You are wonderful, my Pao. I love you very much.

Loc:

My dear, you have been one of the biggest surprises of this whole journey. I met you 6 years ago, and even though we have been estranged for some periods of time, since your knowledge of the incident you have been taking care of me with love and care whenever I allow you to. Thank you for your support and your unconditional care.

Dr. Mena:

You are a being of light, who takes the darkness of our minds and hearts to transform it into hope. You are respectful, you are professional, you have a unique ethic and incomparable value and love for your work. In addition to being a human with values and principles that I have only been able to see in you.

I admire you for the great woman, mother, daughter and professional that you are. You are word and deeds, not just a facade that goes looking for clients. Since the beginning of my sessions with you, thousands of things have changed. I know that there are things that I may never be able to rebuild in their entirety, but you have allowed me to heal and rebuild myself similarly to a kintsugi work of art.

You have taught me to be vulnerable and to take care of myself with love. You have highlighted my values and strengths, even when I can only see the dark. You are a miracle in this world.

Thank you for listening to me, for guiding me, for helping me heal and for your advice. You always give me hope. Your role as a psychologist is so important that I don't think you can imagine how you save our lives every day, because you are a witness and companion to those things that we can only entrust to someone who gives us peace.

Dr. Fabian:

Doctor Fabian, medicine is one of the most beautiful professions. Without a doubt, for people who are going through situations of change, it is the place where we look for hope. You are a wonderful person, your professionalism and dedication to each patient makes us the people who love you, admire and respect you. I am immensely grateful for your arrival in our lives. I sincerely hope that all your projects succeed. The world needs more professionals like you, committed to the well-being of others. Caring for others requires courage and great responsibility, exactly as you demonstrate every day.

Places of Help and Hope

Below you will find a list of different organizations that provide support in extreme situations. These organizations are committed to social welfare and their mission is to help people in need regardless of visa or immigration status; most are non-profit.

This first group of entities helps people in different circumstances such as: Disability, legal support, advice to find a job, refugees with different aspects, food, payment of services, psychological support and studies and other services. It is important to check that it applies to your needs; in case you need support with English, you can call 131450 free interpreter services and request that the entity you need be contacted.

https://www.amparo.org.au/

Contacto: (07) 33544900

https://romerocentre.org.au/

Contacto: (07) 3013 0100

https://worldwellnessgroup.org.au/

Contacto: 1300 079 020

https://www.54reasons.org.au/

Contacto: 1800 874 996

https://qpastt.org.au/

Contacto: (07) 3391 6677

Refugee & Immigration Legal Service

Contacto:

https://www.healthdirect.gov.au/

Contacto: (07) 384 63490

https://www.lwb.org.au/

Contacto: 1800 935 483

Second group: entities that help with food, utility bills, and other things. The organization should be contacted to identify what services they can provide.

https://www.redcross.org.au/
Contacto: 07-33675665

https://indooroopillyuc.org.au/
Contacto:

https://www.vinnies.org.au/
Contacto: 13 18 12

https://www.holyspiritparish.com.au/
Contacto:

https://www.mgcci.org.au/
Contacto: (07) 3343 9833

In case of emergency

Lifeline

13 11 14

HOMELESS HOTLINES

1800474753 24/7 assistance

13 HEALTH

13 43 25 84

Ambulances

000

Human Rights Commission

1300130673

Immigrant Women's Support Service (IWSS)

www.iwss.org.au

Email:

Domestic Violence Program

(07)38463490

Sexual Assault Program

(07)38465400

National Sexual Assault Domestic Violence

And Counselling Service

1800737732 (24 hours)

Kind Helpline

Counselling Services

1800551800

Mental Health Helplines

24/7 Hours 13 11 14, text 0477 13 11 14

Beyond Blue: 24/7 Support for Anxiety, Depression and ...

1300 22 4636

AUTHOR

Francy was born in small town, Colombia in 1986. She is an enterprising, supportive woman focused on social welfare, with different fields of experience that have trained her in business administration, project management, community service, caregiver, holistic life coach, author and writer of the book series The Phoenix Part I, THE PHOENIX RISING Part II.

Constancy, faith, persistence, love, patience and tolerance are the greatest tools to overcome any obstacle in our lives. Never lose hope, behind every test always come wonderful things, trust —"FAB"

SOCIAL MEDIA

https://linktr.ee/thephoenixreawaken

If you want your story to reach others as a message of love, write to me so I can share it in the next volume.

9 780648 613824